HOME

Back again
To the small untidy steamer,
The delay on the wharf,
The fierce blue
And the isle growing nearer.

Back again
To the steep and the slope,
Wide bay and dark inlet
And a league of gold gorse-blocks,
The harbour, the faces
Peering over the wall.

Back again
To the road
That winds upward for ever,
The tinkle of water,
The riot of wild flowers,
Primroses, bluebells, sea-campion
And May trees in bud.

Back again
To the summit,
The white gulls
On the newly-turned fields,
The rough road,
The thatched cottage.

Trevor Blakemore

SARK

by Ken Hawkes

*Au buon monde de Ser . . . puise l'ute île tréjoue r'tenin la
bieauté trantille q'j'trouvis et q'j'aimis, quan j'y vins ya
pus d'quarante ans déjà.*

ISBN 0 902550 46 2

Originally published in Great Britain by David & Charles.

Printing History

David & Charles edition published 1977
The Guernsey Press revised edition published 1983
Reprinted 1987
New revised edition 1992

Published by The Guernsey Press Co. Ltd.,
Braye Road, Vale, Guernsey, C. I.

Made and printed in Great Britain by
The Guernsey Press Co. Ltd., Guernsey, Channel Islands.

CONTENTS

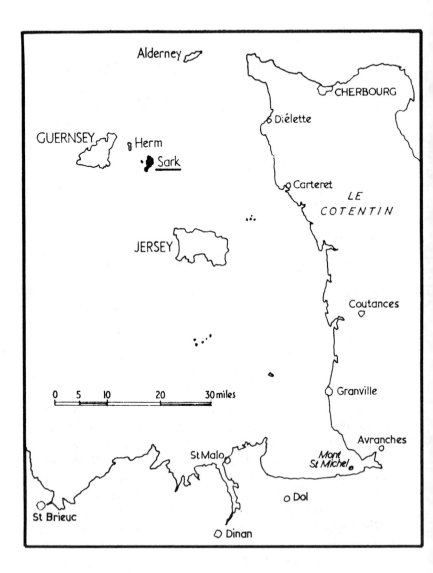

Alderney

CHERBOURG

Diélette

GUERNSEY

Herm

Sark

Carteret

LE COTENTIN

JERSEY

Coutances

0 5 10 20 30 miles

Granville

Avranches

St Malo

Mont St Michel

o Dol

St Brieuc

Dinan

1 SMALL, SWEET WORLD

'Small, sweet world of wave-encompassed wonder'
A. C. Swinburne

SARK's magnificent coastal scenery, lovingly described by poets like Swinburne and drawn or painted by countless artists from J. M. W. Turner to Mervyn Peake, is a source of recurring wonder and delight on each new approach to the island. The charm had more time to work during the leisurely one-hour crossing on the windswept deck of the battered old cargo vessel *Ile de Serk* (formerly *Island Commodore*), which butted her way over from Guernsey for most of the post-war years, until sold in 1982. Now the trip takes only 40 minutes on the enclosed launches *Bon Marin* and *L'Esprit de Serk,* or 45 on the present cargo boat, *Sark Venture.* It was Serk—or Sercq—incidentally, until the 'e' became Anglicised to 'a' at the end of the last century.

Speed is alien here, unless you are beating an unhappy retreat to 'the mainland', as the native Sarkese call England. The slower passage gave a welcome opportunity to adjust to Sark's gentle tempo, though the hour could lengthen uncomfortably in dirty weather. The nine-mile route is usually past the southern flank of Jethou, perhaps setting up a pair of puffins, into the lee of Herm, then out across the Great Russel channel, passing the lone rock of Noire Pute and the islets of the Humps, strung in a line from Galeu and Godin to Grande Amfroque on the port side, and on through foaming cross-currents round Sark's northern tip—unless adverse winds send you 'south-about'.

N

Le Bec du Nez
Pêcheresse
Courbée du Nez
La Grune
Congrière
L'Eperquerie landing
Les
Fontaines Grand
Bay Creux
Les Sept Moies
Noire
Pierre
Le Fort
Petite
Moie
Banquette
landing
BANQUETTE
BAY
Grève
Les Autelets Saigne de la Ville
Bay
Port
du Moulin
Pte
Grande
Tintageu La Robert Moie
Pegane Seigneurie Lighthouse
Port à la Jument
Moie Botarde Moie de La Valette
Mouton Fourimis
Gouliot Maseline Harbour
BRECQHOU Headland Sark à Chapel
Juan +Ch
La Givaude Le Port Le Manoir
Pte Bélème Beauregard Harbour Hill Pinnacle
Moie au La Vaurocque Prison Collenette Creux
Pte à Fouille Sieur Peter Harbour Burons
Havre Gosselin S A R K Les Lâches
Pierre du
Norman Longue S Old Mill
Les Dents Pte Dosdâne Derrible Petit Derrible
Bay
Moie des
Gngeries Derrible
Port és Saies Bay
Pte Château Pte Derrible
Creux D La Conchée
Gardin
La Grande Grève
Pte le Jeu
Convache
Vermandaie Bay Chasm BALEINE
BAY
Moie de La
Fontaine LITTLE SARK Moie
Old Mill Fano
Les Hautes Baleine
Boues Pot Bay
Balmée
Moie de La
Bretagne Pignons
landing
Petite Rouge Terrier
Baveuse Port Gorey La
Silver Brenière
Mines
Grande
Bretagne Pierre du Cours
Moie du
Serçul Viet
Demies

L'Etac

O ¼ ½ ¾ 1 mile
O ½ 1 km

The coastline that looks sombre and barren from Guernsey is gradually transformed. High cliffs take on multi-coloured definition, with a few houses perched on top of brilliant, grass-green and gorse-gold slopes that merge into the reds and greys of the plunging granite. Bays, gullies and caves rend open the west coast and the off-island of Brecqhou detaches itself. The perils of uncharted sailing become obvious as some of the hundreds of jagged rocks ringing Sark are revealed, though most, known as *boues* (Norman French for sunken rocks) lie permanently submerged. Some, like Boue William Baker, Boues Hamon and Boue Philip Guille, carry the names of fishermen whose catches were boosted by their discovery. Not all are hidden. Showing just above water off Brenière islet to the southeast is Boue Américaine, its deep central cleft opened by the prow of an American ship pursued by French pirates. Some sailors killed in the wreck are said to be buried on Brenière, mourned—or mocked—by screaming, wheeling seabirds.

Other rocks are called *moie* (mass) and *grune* (rocky bottom). The word *creux* (hole), sometimes used for caves and gullies, more correctly applies to cliff chimneys, where sea, wind and rain have acted on geological faults to create great shafts, with caves at the base opening to the shore.

LOCATION AND SIZE

Smallest of the four main Channel Islands, beautiful and still unspoiled, Sark has a total area of only 1,348 acres (543ha) between latitude 2°20' and 2°24'W (including off-lying Brecqhou) and longitude 49°24' and 49°27'N (including out-lying L'Etac). The distance from Bec du Nez in the north to Petit Etac in the south is barely 3 miles (4.8km)—not 3½ unless L'Etac, ½ mile offshore, is included. Sark's greatest width is 1½ miles from Gouliot headland in the west to Pointe Cagnons. The island is almost cut in two where the high, narrow neck of La Coupée joins diamond-

9

shaped Great Sark to Little Sark in the south. If property rights did not, in places, bar a complete circuit being made of the 300ft (91m), often sheer cliffs girdling two plateaux of tableland, it would be a walk of some 42 miles (67.5km).

Sark lies 7½ miles (12km) east of Guernsey, 19 miles (30.5km) south of Alderney, 12 miles (19km) north-east of Jersey and 22 miles (35km) west of France. Geographically, like the other Channel Islands, it is indisputably French, tucked in the right-angled Bay of Avranches, between Normandy's Cotentin peninsula and the north coast of Brittany. Politically, by accident of the Norman Conquest, it belongs to the British Crown. Administratively, it is a last relic of feudalism, governed by the Court of Chief Pleas (*Chef Plaids*), whose voting members are the seigneur, or lord of the manor; a presiding *sénéchal* (seneschal), the owners of forty freehold *tènements* (tenements, or holdings) and twelve people's deputies.

BOATS AND CARRIAGES

From spring to October there are frequent boat services from Guernsey, and catamarans from Jersey, with connections from St Malo and Granville in France. In winter, weather permitting, cargo comes twice a week from Guernsey, with boats operating a daily service, apart from Sunday, and longer shopping trips every Wednesday and once a month on Saturday. Since 1969 the Guernsey service has been by the Isle of Sark Shipping Company, in which the island is a 51 per cent shareholder. Launches can be chartered for unscheduled sailing.

There is no airstrip and helicopter landings are generally allowed only when gales makes it impossible to get sick people or animals to Guernsey by sea, though an exception was made for the Queen Mother's visit in May 1975.

News travels fast by bush telegraph, so the 'village', 320ft above sea level, often knows of anyone's arrival before he reaches it, either on foot, sitting in a tractor-drawn trailer, or—though less likely, because few go down the steep hill nowadays—on one of the horse-drawn carriages licensed to carry passengers. There are no cars.

The carriages are Sark's version of 'Any more for the Skylark?' A selection of the five governess carts, five victorias, two dozen 'vans'—used in pre-tractor days to transport goods from the harbour—and 22 waggonettes await trippers at the top of the hill, offering a tour of Great Sark.

The leather-hooded victorias are aristocrats of the carriage trade, always used on ceremonial occasions, as when the Duke of Edinburgh came to the island with Princess Elizabeth in 1949 to open the new harbour. They were driven by the late Charlie Perrée, a well-loved personality who afterwards received permission to put the Edinburgh coat of arms on his victoria. Another carriage, belonging to Johnny de Carteret, which carried the Queen and Prince Philip on their 1957 visit, has the date it was built, 1892, cut into the axle; bought for £60, it is probably now worth £8,000. Old carriages no longer go up in flames on Bonfire Night, rot in farmyards, or get tipped over the cliffs. Their owners have happily realised they are sitting on a small fortune. Some display their skills in the periodic trials of Sark Driving Society, or compete in those on Guernsey and Jersey.

The carriages, a picturesque expression of Sark's leisurely life-style, ironically also reflect transition from a traditional economy of agriculture and fishing to outright reliance on tourism. There is no manufacturing industry.

FARMING AND FISHING

Many old farm buildings have been demolished, stand in roofless ruin, or have been converted to residential use. Once all forty tenements were farms, now only a dozen or so remain. Older farmers nostalgically recall the waving seas of golden wheat and other cereal crops, when Sark grew all its own grain and had a surplus to export, supplied its own cattle food and most of its vegetables, and when the fishermen had their own small-holdings. Oxen were imported from Diélette to work on the yoke, while practically every household fattened a pig to be killed and salted down for the winter. All this less than sixty-five years ago.

Intensive farming last took place during World War II. In 1941, a year after the Germans occupied Sark, its farms produced 250 vergées (1 vergée = 1,960sq yd or 0.4 of an acre) of grain, 111 vergées of root vegetables, 84 of potatoes, 53 of maize and kale, not including much small-scale market gardening.

There has been a marked improvement in the use of farmland during the past ten years, but too much of it is still neglected. The Island paid £5,479 in farming subsidies during 1990.

Most farming is now pastoral, but the 200 or so cattle are often tethered, so fodder can be grown in strips of the same fields. The cows, all pedigree Guernseys, produce rich milk, from which the distinctive deep-yellow Sark butter and cream are made. Milk is bottled and delivered by one of the farms. About one-sixth of the grazing land supports some seventy draught horses for the carriages and there are several flocks of sheep, some pigs, goats, donkeys and poultry.

But catering for visitors brings easier returns than farming—or fishing. In living memory Sark had forty boats: thirty on the moorings at Les Lâches, two at L'Eperquerie, one each at Port du Moulin and Rouge Terrier, the rest at Havre Gosselin. By World War II it was a score, in 1960 a dozen, now only a handful remain; but beautifully finished working boats were, until recent years, occasionally built by one veteran craftsman and his son. Rich catches can still be pulled in the pots, or lifted on the many-hooked trot-lines and Sark's few fishermen make a comfortable, if hard-working, living; although the profitable export trade in dried, salted fish is long forgotten.

POPULATION

The number of residents has varied little for 150 years. Apart from World War II and a short-lived mining boom (785 inhabitants in 1841), the population dropped below 500 only in the 1821 census (488) and topped 600 only in 1921 (611). The figure for 1831 was 543; in April, 1971, there were 590 including visitors and six Brecqhou residents, so the present permanent population can be little more than 500. Sark did not participate in the 1981 or 1991 Censuses. The big changes have been in the people themselves.

Up to the end of World War I English was hardly spoken in the closely knit community with its own language and customs. By 1971 only 247 of the residents were born in the bailiwick of Guernsey, which includes Sark. Within little more than fifty years half the Sarkese had been replaced by immigrants: 199 from the United Kingdom, 17 from Jersey and 30 from elsewhere. At the same time the number of houses had more than doubled from 131 in 1900. Because so many immigrants are elderly refugees from British taxation, an imbalance has resulted in age groupings; of the 590 people in 1971, 270 were more than fifty years of age.

Immigrants now own about half the forty tenements and the score of other freehold properties. Not all have made any positive return for their privileges. In general they do not mix on equal terms with the Sarkese, who understandably, if belatedly, resent ownership having passed from local hands when the going rate for a tenement was a small fraction of the £275,000 a freehold property fetched recently.

The divide was noted by two 'foreign' residents. French-born vicar J. L. V. Cachemaille wrote in 1874: 'In Sark, the people work if they choose . . . they must have their chat with the passer-by, or maybe smoke a pipe . . . nothing could be less reliable or more irregular than the Sark labourer.' Sixty years later an English ex-army captain Ernest Platt considered 'the Sarkese . . . have acquired the art of carefully guarding their innermost thoughts . . . it is impossible to break down the barrier which exists between the Sarkese and the English'.

That 'barrier', perhaps economic rather than ethnic, is more easily overcome by working immigrants, themselves divided between seasonal labour for the hotels and carriages and those who make the island their permanent home. The latter often marry into Sark families and some see their children also marry native islanders, so the third generation become three-quarter Sarkese. More than half the fifty or so schoolchildren, however, have not even one Sark-born parent.

SOCIAL SERVICES

Sark society rests firmly on a basis of mutual aid and voluntary effort that maintains social services such as the fire brigade. Since 1969, the part-time, elected constables (*connétable* and *vingtenier*) have been supplemented during the holiday season by a uniformed policeman from Guernsey, which charges for his services—and the upkeep of Sark prisoners in its jail. The 1990 accounts showed £2,500 and £816 respectively against these items, the latter an indication of the happily low incidence of crime. The policemen and constables sometimes refuse landing permission to known undesirables, but visitors generally get a courteous, friendly welcome.

Health

The resident medical officer, who is paid a retaining salary by Chief Pleas and provided with a house, charges for consultations, as there is no health or unemployment insurance. Prescriptions are met from the fund based on the legacy of a late tenant, Professor C. F. M. Saint. Cases needing surgery or nursing care reach Guernsey by the fast ambulance launch, *Flying Christine II,* manned by St John Ambulance volunteers, having been taken to one of the harbours in the tractor-drawn caravan which, some years ago, replaced a boxlike horse ambulance reminiscent of the Crimean War. In recent years, private medical insurance for all, paid for by residents, was forced on Sark by Guernsey's decision to charge UK private hospital rates for Sark patients.

Care of the children's teeth is paid for from a special fund started by the late Dame Sibyl Hathaway, Sark's ruler for forty-seven years. Well over £1,000 was raised on her ninetieth birthday in January 1974, when she insisted on donations, not presents. Later that year there were only family flowers at her funeral and other mourners sent further contributions. There is no resident dentist or optician, so a trip to Guernsey must be made to obtain treatment.

Education

Free, co-educational classes for infants, juniors and seniors are conducted by three full-time teachers with part-time assistance. At the age of eleven about a third of the pupils go either to Elizabeth College in Guernsey or boarding school in England; their tuition and, in cases of need, board are paid for by the island. Students qualifying for university have been given grants by the Island. Children who stay in Sark leave school at fifteen or, at latest, sixteen. In 1990 £21,561 was paid in teachers' salaries and pension contributions, £14,735 in scholarship fees and expenses, and £7,423 in running costs at the two schools. The teachers are housed by the Island.

Care of the elderly

Needy old people receive a non-contributory weekly pension, administered by the *Procureur des Pauvres* and *Douzaine*—Chief Pleas' senior, twelve-strong committee— from the only direct tax, levied by guesswork assessment of all permanent residents' property and capital. This is reckoned in 'quarters'—units originally based on quarter measures of corn—and the amount of tax per quarter is fixed by Michaelmas Chief Pleas. Collection is made by the constables. In 1990 the tax was fixed at £1 a quarter and the pension at £50 a week. From tax revenue of £64,230 in 1989-90, £37,000 was paid in pensions and £1,921.90 in fuel subsidies to pensioners. The account was £50,000 in credit.

Up to the 1930s people seeking relief had their applications publicly posted and their goods and chattels could be sold. Now the douzeniers, who usually know individual circumstances, arrange things tactfully and the stigma of the poor law has gone.

Old folk in need of permanent care, however, must leave their homes for Guernsey. Some years ago the tenement of Ville Roussel was left to the island by the Major Timothy Breen, for use as an old people's home. The property stood empty for some years after his death and was then sold to a private English buyer, with the island retaining about half its land and establishing a building site for Sark persons in one field. Part of the sale proceeds was later made available for loans to those allowed to build homes there.

Water, waste and power

There is no mains water or drainage. Tanks catch rain off the roofs; there are many old wells, and some modern boreholes reach a table of sparkling water at depths from 80 to 140ft (24-43m). Tanks can be refilled by watercart, for which the current charge is £10 per 500 gallons.

The six hotels and most of the larger houses have septic tanks for sewage disposal; others use earth soak-aways or cesspits. There have been no serious epidemics since an isolated outbreak of typhoid fever in the 1920s. Visitors sometimes get short-lived attacks of 'Sark tummy', from which residents are usually immune.

Waste disposal on Great Sark is by burying or burning, and by tipping non-combustible rubbish over the wall at the foot of Harbour Hill, to be carried away by the tide. The age of plastic and non-returnable glass containers has created problems, with unsightly refuse washed up in the bays, but Little Sark's waste disappears neatly down disused Prince's mineshaft.

An efficient mains power supply has been provided by the privately owned Electric Supply Company since 1948 and there are a few independent generators. Cylinder gas is widely used for cooking, oil and coal for heating. Freightage of fuel to the Island helps raise lighting and heating costs well above those in the UK and Guernsey. This is generally true of necessities, including food; only luxury goods, such as cosmetics, radios, cameras and television sets, where no VAT is payable, or spirits and tobacco, on which local tax is appreciably lower than UK excise duty, cost less than in Britain.

Road maintenance and transport

Maintenance of the public roads is the responsibility of the connétable, who receives funds from Chief Pleas (£12,600 in 1990) for repairs and improvements. Foundations are of stone, with a top dressing of granite chippings and dirt, which gets badly cut up by tractors. These noisily mock the ban on cars, as they smother hedges, houses and pedestrians with dust.

Before World War II transport was by mule, donkey and horse-drawn vehicle, by cycle or on foot. Dame Sibyl afterwards established her own right—later granted to other disabled people—to an invalid carriage, electrically propelled at a silent 5mph. Tractors, introduced for farming, gradually extended their scope to carting, then general business use and finally became the easy way of shopping or just getting around. From a handful in 1950 they snowballed to thirty-five in 1965 and sixty-three in 1990—one for every seventh adult.

Legislation passed in 1974 checked their numbers, by restricting licences to business use and insisting that new applications conform with this condition as old machines wear out. But 'business use' leaves many loopholes. Some islanders and many visitors, remembering the formerly peaceful roads, believe fifteen tractors used communally could comfortably service Sark's needs. Bicycles increased even more sharply, from about thirty before World War II to 1,187 in 1990; they can be hired by visitors for the day, or weekly.

Island income

Licence fees for tractors (£20), tractor drivers (£1), carriages (£3 to £10, according to size), carriage drivers (£1), dogs and cycles (each £1), boats (£1), and hawkers (£5) are collected by the constables and held in a 'Local Account'. This covers such items as maintenance of the harbour toilets and crane, trimming and planting trees and rat poison. The Account was almost £3,000 in credit in 1990.

The main source of income is an *impôt* on alcoholic drinks, tobacco and a few other items, which netted £88,408 in 1990. With £56,848 from the landing tax of 75p paid by each non-resident adult—a poll tax originally levied to pay off the loan raised to build Maseline Harbour, but since 1978, when this was achieved, part of the general budget income; £41,446 from investment income, £20,603 from usage of the harbour crane, £4,409 from import duties and agricultural levies and £15,102 from other sources, the 1990 income was £226,816 against expenditure of £178,102. Sark's total assets and investments in its General Account were £658,470, more than double the 1981 figure, and a remarkably healthy state of financial affairs for such a small community.

2   THE POEM IN STONE

'. . . *le plus merveilleux poème de pierres
qui surgisse de la surface des eaux*'
Victor Hugo

TOPOGRAPHICALLY Sark is an erosion plateau, its magnificent coastline sculptured by marine action, which has picked out the many geological faults and dykes to form caves, tunnels, deep gullies, bays and the steep, sometimes perpendicular, cliffs. From the sea it appears rugged, almost barren; only on reaching the high tableland does a patchwork pattern unfold of small fields *(clos or clôtures)* enclosed by hedges and earth banks, with a few areas of open common and woodland.

The soil, generally fine and quick-draining, thins at the extremities: L'Eperquerie common, helmeted with gorse and heather in the north; balding cliffs around Gouliot headland to the west; the rocky outcrops of Pointe Derrible and Pointe Château in the east; the bared granite at—and off—the southern tip of Little Sark.

Woodland is found mainly in sheltered hollows, most extensively around La Seigneurie, on Harbour Hill, above Petit Dixcart and from Dixcart Valley to Rue de la Coupée. Surface water is confined to small ponds at La Seigneurie, Beauregard and Dixcart Farm, a dewpond above Derrible Bay and tiny streams running to the sea down such coastal valleys as those above Port du Moulin and Grève de la Ville, or bordering Harbour Hill. Sadly, as elsewhere, many trees were felled by the hurricanes of recent years, removing much welcome shelter.

CLIMATE

The climate is similar to that of Guernsey, generally warm and sunny in summer and mild in winter, with frost and snow so rare that geraniums happily survive outdoors and dahlias do not need to be lifted. There is usually a cooling sea breeze on the hottest days and the air is cleanly invigorating. A medical research project in 1973 established that, due to the absence of petrol exhaust fumes, Sark air has only one part per million of toxic carbon monoxide, compared with twenty parts per million at Smithfield Market, London. Sea mist, dense enough to reduce visibility to a few yards, is fairly common and sometimes persistent. But the skies are very often clear of cloud, stars seem to shine with extraordinary brilliance and thunderstorms coming from the south or south-west reputedly divide to miss Sark, one half passing over Jersey, the other across Guernsey.

THE ROADS

Sark's seven-plus miles of dusty road, mostly public but with a few privately maintained stretches, are bordered by earth banks and hedges thick with honeysuckle, generally following the lines of their original construction four centuries ago. They vary in width from 6ft lanes to the 20ft of Harbour Hill.

Amont du Creux and the village

The road from the two east-coast harbours of Maseline and Creux, Amont du Creux or, more commonly, Harbour Hill, is an exception to the straight-line rule, winding up a wooded valley carpeted in season with primroses, bluebells and Cornish moneywort, past the island quarry, Aval du Creux hotel, the power station and Bel Air tavern (open at 10 am) to La Collenette (or Collinette) crossroads. It continues as The Avenue, named when it was an elegant, tree-shaded driveway to the old seigneurie of Le Manoir, but now the shopping centre and dustily reminiscent of the American Wild West.

The village is not among Sark's many beauties. A dozen shops catering for the needs of residents and visitors, two banks, cafés, post office with Sark's only pillar box, shanties of wood and corrugated iron, some presentable modern structures and attractive old granite buildings form a piecemeal conglomeration along The Avenue and Rue Lucas.

The Avenue forks left at the post office to Le Manoir, which faces the junior school, two-cell prison and former militia arsenal, then becomes Rue du Moulin. The right fork passes the Greffe office to join La Chasse Marette, a road from Le Manoir past the vicarage, St Peter's Church, the cemetery, Island Hall and senior school to the crossroads at Clos à Jaon (gorse field).

The church, built in 1820 at a cost of £1,000, had its chancel and tower added in the 1880s, when the bell was cast in France from two six-pounder brass field guns, a legacy of the recent disbanded militia. More than 100 years ago D.T.Ansted and R. C. Latham wrote in *The Channel Islands* that the church 'in its original naked ugliness . . . produces a most disagreeable effect'. It seems a harsh judgement on this unpretentious granite building.

To the south of La Collenette, with Jersey's sandy northern bays shining brightly ahead on a sunny day, Rue de la Peigneurie bends left to the cottages of that name and on to La Forge, once a blacksmith's shop, Derrible and Les Lâches. A private road with pedestrian access, below the National Westminster Bank, cuts west towards Baker's and Dixcart valleys; a lane at La Peigneurie dips to Petit Dixcart. Tennis courts and a riding school are on the right, just below the bank.

Rue Lucas and Rue Hotton

North from La Collenette, Rue Lucas, named after sixteenth-century tenant Lucas Le Masurier, passes the Greffe Office on the way to Le Carrefour crossroads. A recently demolished little cottage to the left, Old Place, housed the Midland Bank which is now in purpose-built premises across the road; a sign in the window read: 'This office will be open every Tuesday, 11.30 to 3.0, circumstances permitting,' because bad weather meant no boat or bank clerk from Guernsey.

The Greffe Office is in the old telephone exchange, closed when Sark switched to subscriber trunk dialling at 8 am on June 6 1979. Previously you wound a handle to raise the operator, asked for your free local call by the name of the subscriber and possibly learnt he or she was on a shopping trip to Guernsey! Most houses now have a phone and there are four public ones.

Rue Hotton, also named after a former tenant, leaves Rue Lucas by La Marguerite cottage (1610) and passes the Mermaid tavern, a centre for dances, darts and whist drives to reach rebuilt La Valette, one of Sark's old houses. Pointe Robert lighthouse lies ahead, tucked in the cliff down a long flight of steps, with its breathtaking, bird's-eye view of La Grande Moie. The lighthouse, which can be visited by arrangement with its Trinity House keepers, was built in 1912 and the electrically-powered, $2^1/_4$ million candlepower light, flashing four times a minute and visible for 21 miles, has substantially reduced danger to shipping east of Sark. It will probably go automatic in 1992.

Rue Pôt and Rue du Sermon

Rue Pôt goes east from Le Carrefour to Ville Roussel and a T-junction; the left turn goes down a dip to one of Sark's oldest cottages, where a typical long house was formed by extending the original single-storeyed, two-room frontage. A nearby well has supplied the tenement of Ville Roussel de

23

bas since Elizabethan days. The right turn of the 'T' leads to another delightful, sleepy group of dwellings at La Ville, then to a field often used for camping at the top of the path to Grève de la Ville, with a rough road right joining Rue Hotton.

From Le Carrefour and past Clos à Jaon to the corner by the Methodist chapel runs Rue du Sermon. The name is shown on some maps as applying only as far as Clos à Jaon; it may date from when Elie Brévint, seventeenth-century diarist-vicar, made his Sunday morning walks from Clos de la Ville to deliver warnings of hellfire in the Presbyterian Temple at Le Manoir.

Rue de la Vieille Cimetière

Sometimes Brévint's footsteps in the line of duty must have continued to the old burial ground beside the present Methodist chapel, where gravestones, now mostly illegible, bear surnames no longer found in Sark: Le Pelley, Gascoigne, Slowley, Godfray, Mollet, Le Malnier, Dumaresq.

The chapel has been there since the late Duncan Henderson, then tenant of Ville Roussel, objected to the full-throated French singing which emanated from crowded Wesleyan services at the galleried meeting-place near his house. He gave the Methodists a parcel of land well away from dwellings and they were granted freehold by special dispensation of the Privy Council. When the chapel was demolished, with a row of charming old cottages, two of the trustees, Thomas Remphrey and P. T. Carré, removed its 150 tons of stone by horse and box-cart to the new site. The £2,993 14s 2d cost of rebuilding had been paid off when the chapel opened in 1925, but the move heralded a decline in Methodist membership from virtually half the islanders (the others were Anglican) to the sad 1982 figure of some half-a-dozen.

The main road turns south, as Rue de la Vieille Cimetière *(Chimtire* in patois) to La Vaurocque (formerly Veau

24

Rocque) crossroads, while a rough cart track continues west to Port à la Jument, then south-west to Le Petit Champ hotel and the eighteenth-century farmhouse of Le Vieux Port.

Rue de Beauregard

A right rurn at La Vaurocque, Rue de Beauregard, leads to the duckpond, Beauregard hotel and its Barn Bar, where the landlord was reputed to make a law-abiding gesture of shutting the top half of the divided door after calling 'Time'.

Opposite Beauregard a track descends from the modern guesthouse, La Fregondée, to the original cottage of that name. This was made the heroine's retreat in Hesba Stretton's Victorian romance, *The Doctor's Dilemma,* to the irritation of its fisherman owner, continually pestered by curious visitors.

Another cottage facing the hotel is notable because apart from the enlargement of windows, addition of mortar and loss of its thatch, the original form of sixteenth-century construction has been retained. It is 25ft (7m) long, 17ft (5m) deep and only 6ft 6in (2m) from ground to eaves, solid and four-square.

Rue de Moulin

Eastwards from La Vaurocque is Rue du Moulin, leading back to Le Manoir past the landmark of the old seigneurial mill at one of the highest points in the Channel Islands, shown on the last survey map made for the Ministry of Defence in 1965 as 356ft (109m) above mean sea level at the St Peter Port gauge. The mill provides extensive views seaward, and visible at night are the flashing navigation lights of the Casquets, Quenard (Alderney), St Martin's Point, St Peter Port and Platte Fougère (Guernsey), Corbière and Grosnez (Jersey), Cap de la Hague, Carteret and Diélette (France) and the Roches Douvres.

SARK

Described by Dame Sibyl as the 'oldest stone-built windmill in the British Empire', the 1571 building was brought out of retirement to supply Sark with good flour during World War I and finally ceased turning in 1919, its last miller being the white-bearded Jim Hamon. In World War II, the two remaining sails and the roof were dismantled by the Germans to make a look-out; afterwards the roof was restored, but attempts to have the sails replaced more recently came to nothing.

Rue de la Coupée and Little Sark

Rue de la Coupée, from La Vaurocque to the narrow land bridge that links with Little Sark, passes Happy Valley and the hamlet of Dosdâne (Dos d'Ane, donkey's back) above Port és Saies on the right, with Dixcart Lane tunnelling down through trees on the left to Stock's and Dixcart hotels, and La Jaspellerie on the cliffs beyond.

Despite its ugly iron railing and concreted road—built in 1945 by German prisoners-of-war under Royal Engineers' direction—the 100yd-long, 260ft-high knife-edge of La Coupée, Sark's most spectacular feature, can still be frightening to cross in a gale. Before 1900, when a protective railing was first put up, traversing this ridge of clay and decomposed rock must have been terrifying for anyone afraid of heights. Sometimes the children of Little Sark, going to school on the other side, had to crawl over on hands and knees. Surprisingly, there are only two recorded fatalities. Tenant Philippe Hamon was blown to his death in 1731, while carrying a tithe of corn for Dame Le Pelley; and Danny Lanahan, an Irishman working in Little Sark, overbalanced from the railing during an April night in 1975. Both went over the sheerer east side.

A landslide in 1811 reduced the width of the roadway to less than a stride at one point; another fall in 1862 led to the construction of a partial retaining wall on the west. Near beach level on the west side at that time there was a small meadow, used for grazing donkeys. Erosion has since completely destroyed it. Standing on La Coupée you may, if the wind is right, hear the sound of mourning voices from La Cave des Lamentations in Little Sark's east coast. During the Occupation, German soldiers moved an abandoned bungalow to the cliff edge above the cave, for use as a look-out. The Sarkese awaited the inevitable and one night a south-west gale swept it to destruction on the rocks below.

Across the Coupée, La Veineraise goes towards La Sablonnerie hotel, forking left there past a café and tea garden on its way to the old silver mines and barracks, or straight on to Duval Farm and La Duvallerie—the end of the road south and Sark at its peaceful best.

La Grande Rue de l'Eperquerie

Sark's northern end is reached by two roads. From Clos à Jaon, La Grande Rue de l'Eperquerie is divided, for Sarkese conversational convenience, into three short sections: l'Premi Frêne (first ash tree), Rue de la Seigneurie and Rue de l'Esprectie.

La Seigneurie stands to the west of the road in spacious grounds, shielded by a high stone wall and ornamental wrought-iron gates presented to Dame Sibyl and her American second husband on their marriage in 1929.

The generally attractive building, in part 400 years old, was extended by the Le Pelley seigneurs and later by Dame Sibyl's grandfather, who added an ugly central tower for signalling to Guernsey. Dame Sibyl, who loathed the tower, unfortunately found the cost of its removal prohibitive.

When her grandson inherited the seignory in 1974, much of the twelve-bedroomed house was in sad disrepair from long disuse. Among many attractive features surviving undisturbed is a fine *Victorian* carved fireplace, not *Elizabethan* as claimed by Dame Sibyl.

The site of the house was that of St Magloire's monastery, dating from the sixth century, and some ancient masonry

27

can be seen in the cellars. A late 18th century chapel, with part of one wall of much earlier construction, is nearby. About 20 x 30ft (6 x 9m) in size, it was used for family services up to the late 19th century, but is now a storeroom. A Dame Sibyl-fostered legend says a collapsed underground passage in the Seigneurie cellars linked them to the monastery proper and that a rich cache of Le Pelley silver, hidden during the Napoleonic Wars, lies buried in it. Michael Beaumont ('More's the pity') has found no trace of either.

A 25ft wall at right angles to the front of the house is probably of early medieval construction to a height of about 8ft; above that is far more recent, perhaps part of the old fortifications. About a quarter of the earthbound wall recently collapsed, because of extreme weather damage. The attractive triple arch to the gardens is relatively modern.

The beautifully-tended gardens are open to the public on Tuesdays to Fridays during the season. An irrigation system introduced by Mr and Mrs Beaumont, has made it possible to replant all the beds, most with a colour scheme, and make extensive use of annuals. Previously the only watering was by can. An ornate *colombier* (dovecote) dates from 1855. Among ordnance in the battery is a brass cannon with the inscription: *Don de Sa Majesté la Royne Elizabeth au Seigneur de Sercq AD 1572*.

Rue de la Moinerie skirts the south and west boundaries of the gardens, leading to a hotel of that name, its bar in a newly renovated period cottage. The main road continues to L'Eperquerie common and, becoming a track, to Sark's original landing.

Rue du Fort and Rue des Camps

The other route north is Rue du Fort, from Le Carrefour to La Tour, then on to Grand Fort and a cluster of cottages and farm buildings, from which a path descends to

Banquette landing. Rue des Camps, the left turn at La Tour, joins Rue de l'Eperquerie at a heart-shaped patch of grass in the road, Le Coeur. Much information about the Island can be gained on Pat Webb's escorted walks during the season.

OLD DWELLINGS

Few old cottages and farmhouses remain in their original structure. In the sixteenth century the high cost of mortar made dry-stone building the Sark rule; surviving in outhouses, barns and ruins, this method is still used for boundary walls by a few old craftsmen. There are no records to show whether dwellings were subsequently pointed, or whether they were demolished and rebuilt with the same stone, as was recently done with cottages dating from 1719 at Clos à Jaon. The last thatched roof, at Le Fort, was removed in the 1960s. Some old houses are now roofed with tiles or slates, but many have corrugated iron—'Sark thatch'.

The first house walls were 4ft thick—an over-cautious insurance against storms sweeping across the plateau on which they were built. As families and prosperity grew, many houses were enlarged and, on the death of a tenant and inheritance of the tenement by his heir, a dower house was often built for the widow.

The original house at L'Ecluse forms part of the present holiday apartments. Clos de la Ville, built as a vicarage, has been greatly extended from its original 30 x 18ft (9 x 5m), both laterally and by rooms with dormer windows in the typical, steeply-pitched roof providing an upper storey. The latter method of expansion is still common, as at La Corderie which dates from 1691. Dwellings were often built to the very edge of the roads, to conserve every inch of land for agriculture.

During the eighteenth century a two-storeyed style, similar to that of Jersey, was adopted for such houses as Ville Farm, Port à la Jument and Clos du Normand.

The older houses are all of Channel Island stone, some quarried locally or taken from the fabric of medieval ruins, the rest imported from Jersey and Guernsey—Jersey's warm, pink tinge contrasts with Guernsey's colder bluish hue.

GEOLOGY

Western Normandy, Brittany and the Channel Islands form an area of igneous, metamorphic and sedimentary rocks, mainly of Precambrian (700 million years) age and known as the Armorican Massif.

Sark is composed of metamorphic and igneous rocks, to be seen mainly in the cliffs, with few inland exposures. The first impression is of flat-lying layers of light- and dark-coloured crystalline rocks. Some were originally sedimentary, possibly volcanic, but folding and deformation during metamorphism make it unlikely that the present layering is the original one. As the layers form a structural succession, rocks now at the bottom, or at sea level, are not necessarily the oldest, as would be the case in an undisturbed pile of sediments.

The island's geology has been described by several workers, among them Hill (1887), Hill and Bonney (1892), Wooldridge (1925), Plymen (1926), Sutton and Watson (1957) and Gibbons (1975). Sutton and Watson recognised a rock succession in which the lowest members are gneisses derived from granites exposed at Creux Harbour and Port à la Jument. These are succeeded by hornblende schists and gneisses—perhaps originally volcanic rocks—and by mica schists and granulites, representing metamorphosed sediments. Within the hornblende schists and near their base are some rounded bodies of serpentinite up to 20ft (6m) long, perhaps produced by the metamorphism and deformation of an ultrabasic igneous rock.

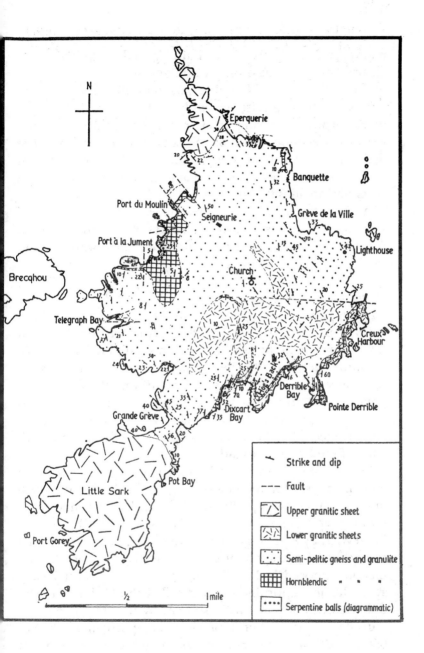

Strike and dip

--- Fault

Upper granitic sheet

Lower granitic sheets

Semi-pelitic gneiss and granulite

Hornblendic

Serpentine balls (diagrammatic)

SARK

Between L'Eperquerie and Banquette the rocks are markedly folded; elsewhere faulting makes the folds less clearly visible. A mass of granitic gneiss occurs within the schists at Dixcart and Derrible bays; both this and the lower, Creux Harbour gneiss probably represent granitic rocks metamorphosed during or after intrusion. Northern Sark, western Brecqhou and most of Little Sark consist of a less deformed, but still foliated granite; at all its contacts this can be seen to overlie the metamorphic rocks and almost certainly intrudes them.

Sark's metamorphic rocks in some ways resemble those of southern Guernsey and, to a lesser extent, western Alderney, while comparisons have been made with rocks in the Lizard area of Cornwall.

Pentevrian or Cadomian?

Investigating the ages of Channel Island rocks, Adams (1967) used methods based on the rate of decay of radioactive elements, which occur in small, but measurable quantities in minerals. The two most important changes are the conversion of rubidium to strontium (Rb–Sr) and of potassium to argon (K–Ar). Interpreting such observations is not straightforward, particularly when an old rock has been subjected to later metamorphism, as is the case with parts of the Channel Islands.

The Rb–Sr method indicates two main periods of metamorphism for the Guernsey gneisses: 2,620 and 1,960 million years (my) ago. Rocks which underwent their main metamorphism more than 900my ago are known as Pentevrian by French geologists, to distinguish them from a younger group, mainly of sedimentary and volcanic rocks, metamorphosed in late Precambrian times, about 700my ago. This metamorphic event is called the Cadomian. The only determinations on Sark rocks by the Rb–Sr method indicate, though rather imprecisely, an approximate date of 650my. Although the Sark rocks resemble the Pentevrian

Plate 1 Brecqhou, with Jethou and Herm behind, from Little Sark *(John Morton, 1904)*

Plate 2 La Grève de la Ville, with La Chapelle és Mauves in the background above the pile of boulders *(M. P. Joyner)*

Plate 3 Grand Derrible Bay, with the clifftop opening to Sark's finest *creux* in the centre of the picture

Plate 4 Gorey Souffleur working in a south-westerly gale

Plate 5 The big *Courier* in full dress, when she made a triumphant return from war work to Guernsey in 1946

Plate 6 Carriages waiting in line for visitors at Creux Harbour—but nowadays the ascent of steep Harbour Hill is usually made in a tractor-drawn trailer

Plate 7 La Seigneurie, part of which dates from the sixteenth century *(M. P. Joyner)*

Plate 8 Now ruined, the guardhouse on L'Eperquerie was home for a family of ten until World War II

Guernsey gneisses in their general appearance and high metamorphic grade, a Cadomian metamorphic date therefore remains possible.

Faulting and minerals

Many nearly vertical basic dykes, up to 40ft (12m) thick, intrude the metamorphic rocks and foliated granites. An older set tends roughly NW–SE and a younger set NE–SW. There are also acid dykes up to 20ft (6m) thick and younger dykes of mica camprophyre. Numerous faults displace the rocks, most with only a small throw. Some faults predate the basic dykes, while others displace these intrusions.

Some faults in Little Sark gave access to solutions from which minerals of economic importance were deposited. Mineral veins were known in Sark in 1609, but mining activity began only in the 1830s (see p116). The principal silver ores present are cerargyrite and argentite, together with pyrargyrite and the antimony-bearing mineral, jamesonite. The chief copper ore is chalcopyrite, which oxidises to malachite and azurite. Calcite is the main gangue mineral and among many other minerals reported from the mines are quartz, feldspar, limonite, wad, pyrite, pyrrbotine, galena, argentiferous galena, stibnite, mispickel and leadhillite.

Amethystine quartz is commonly sold by Channel Island jewellers under the name 'Sarkstone'. Pale amethyst has been recorded from Sark, but the deeply coloured amethysts are not of local origin.

Several raised beaches, about 26ft (8m) above mean sea level, were identified by Gibbons during 1975 in caves and gullies at the island's northern and southern extremities.

3   ROUND THE BOTTOM

'Below, blue drowsy waters lap the shore
On which the rugged headland crouches prone'
Trevor Blakemore

THE COASTS

FOR exploring the coast clockwise either by boat or, for most of its 42 miles on a series of rock scrambles—'going round the bottom', as the islanders call it—Creux Harbour is an ideal point of departure.

Creux Harbour

Landlocked in La Baie de la Motte, this is sometimes described as the world's most beautiful harbour and, wrongly, as the smallest; it is a favourite spot for the Sarkese to laze away sunny Sunday afternoons. The sandy tidal basin dries completely on Spring tides; the little beach, reached through the old tunnel or down a slipway at the entrance to the newer one, has a freshwater spring, Le Robinet (tap), and the reddish-brown, broom-capped cliffs of La Falaise à Génét form a dramatic backcloth.

Before the present breakwater was built in the 1880s, storm-force seas sucked a cutter moored in Creux through the harbour mouth, then hurled it back undamaged, *over* the old wall.

Guarding the southward-facing harbour mouth to the east lie the humped, green islets of Les Bûrons, the most westerly La Chimnée, the highest (65ft) Les Auquets. They recall an old song of Guernsey mariners bound for France: 'La Grande Amfroque par les Bûrons, les bouteilles san bouchons' (Once the Bûrons are in line with Grande Amfroque, we can uncork our bottles). Between them and Sark runs Le Goulet (gullet), where the low-water tide sets strongly to the south and passage north has been forbidden, following a collision. North of the harbour the little headland of Pointe Moitelle ends in the rocks of Les Quards and the higher mark of Pinnacle.

Les Lâches to Pointe Derrible

Southwards round Pointe à Join, easily reached by a path from Harbour Hill, is Les Lâches landing with its moie (rock mass), Pierre Carré and La Four cave, and the fishing boats moored offshore, Creux à Aplais gully north of the landing, like Creux Malzar and Creux Brown just to the south, may have been chimneys before their seaward walls collapsed. The lofty Cathedral Cave can be reached by wading at very low springs *(grandes marées)*, but is best seen by boat; near by is Platon à Môle, a flat rock expanse uncharacteristic of Sark.

Ahead lie Noir Creux and Petit Derrible bay, accessible from the clifftop only to locally guided climbers, with the gloomy Dungeon Cave in the headland left of the bay. Long, rugged Pointe Derrible (Old French: fallen mass of rock) looks uncannily like a prehistoric monster crouched in the sea, its square snout of Le Viquet always threatening to rise and snap up white-capped La Conchée rock $1\frac{1}{2}$ cables ESE, or Les Haises close inshore.

Grand Derrible

A fine complex of caves, Les Ponchettes, pierce the point. Their exit can be reached by scrambling at low springs from the foot of the cliff path to Derrible (correctly Grand Derrible) bay. Directions are in the *Latrobe Guide;* written by two brothers after spending three holidays in Sark before World War I, it is still the best key to beauties unsuspected by followers of well-trodden paths.

Derrible's low-tide sand provides excellent bathing, particularly when its crystal water is not petrol-filmed by the outboard-powered dinghies of yachtsmen too lazy to row or swim ashore. A double entry leads to awesome Creux du Derrible, a giant chimney 80ft (24m) in diameter rising sheer to the clifftop, where you can peer over the lip to watch high water grinding sand and shingle 200ft (61m) below.

A little local dog marooned there in 1974 alerted a rescue party with its terrified barking, but the sea was too rough for their boat to reach the cave; baker Denis le Goubin swam in, repeatedly battered against the walls, and nursed the dog on a rock for several hours, until the boat could reach them. His bravery deserved a better reward than the dog's death from heart failure. Ironically, the chimney's old name was Creux à Chien (dog's hole).

Hog's Back and Dixcart Bay

The aptly named Hog's Back separates Derrible from its southern neighbour, Dixcart, formerly d'Icart or Dicart and sometimes unkindly dubbed the Margate of Sark, because easy access down a gentle valley path makes it in season the most populous bay.

Good rock fishing and a cave penetrating Pointe Château at the end of the Hog's Back are reached by climbing down from beyond an old cannon embedded in the clifftop. Near the cannon is a flat platform where the French fort, Château des Quénevêts, commanded Sark's eastern approaches.

Dixcart Bay has a fine rock arch and one of the island's longest caves, its entrance hidden by a tall, detached rock and penetrating 125 yd (114m) to a circular chamber.

A rewarding cliff walk to La Coupée forks left from the well-worn but pretty path up the wooded valley. Far below are inaccessible, rocky Noire Baie; Dixcart Souffleur, where strong south-easterlies produce a towering spout of spray, as built-up pressure in a small, domed cavern forces the sea back through its entrance, and Pigeons Cave or Creux sur les Pendants.

Convache Chasm to Le Creux à Pôt

A difficult climb from the clifftop north of La Coupée descends to majestic Convache (or Convanche) Chasm, with its towering entrance, needle's-eye exit and deep, blue water. Sunlight reveals every shade of blue in Sark waters, from sapphire to deep indigo, with greens that include the vivid jade of still rock pools.

Rarely visited La Coupée bay, stony and forbidding, lies under the tumbling east face of the land bridge. Southwards of the bay's shoulder, Droti Emanuel, Little Sark's shoreline can be seen only by boat past Monts Razeur bay to the impassable gully at Petite and Grande Moies Fano. Formerly shown on maps as Fannou, this bird roost and hatchery is one of many place-names with alternative spellings, probably because Sark French is unwritten.

It can be reached by scrambling north past the Three Brothers rocks from Creux à Pôt's exit tunnel. Usually known as the Pot and, after Derrible, Sark's most impressive chimney, it is descended down a zigzag, shale path. Adits opened by mining can be seen just north of the sea entrance and halfway up the cliffs.

Verdigris stains, one high patch known a Le Taque à Copper, show the continued presence of minerals, and quartz crystals are found at sea level. Offshore are the rocks of Baleine, which gives its name to Baleine bay, the overall sweep from Pointe Derrible to Brenière; and its half-tide neighbours, Balmée, Demie de Balmée and Avocat, with La Gripe $1/2$ mile to the east.

Brenière and L'Etac

Southwards again Les Pignons landing and Rouge Terrier (or Terrié), are reached from the clifftop garden of le Clôture de Bas, where barracks built during the Napoleonic wars have been converted to an attractive freehold dwelling.

A narrow gully below Rouge Terrier, which dries at low tide, separates the islet of Moie de la Brenière, itself riven in two with an arch in the outer section. Brenière is also known as Lady's Slipper, its exact shape when seen from the Hog's Back.

Some 40-50ft (12-15m) above sea level in Brenière bay, south of the islet, a patch of stonework suggests early fortifications not mentioned in historical research and there is a similar survival above Banquette landing in Great Sark. Strange shapes and markings scar the rocks, a huge butterfly being one notable example. Rock pools abound, with Venus in the south-west corner of Clouet bay the one most visited. Given its name by William A.Toplis, an artist who first painted Sark in Victorian times and died there in 1942, this circular pool with 18ft (5.4m) of translucent water forms a perfect natural bath, cleansed at every high tide. The pool was partially filled by a bad rock fall during the 1990-1 winter.

Off Sark's most southerly point, Petit Etac at the end of Pointe à Clouet, is Jupiter's Pool and, two gullies further on, Gorey Souffleur, which works in the south-westerlies that helped shape this wild rock landscape. Near by is the Teddy Bath, a deep round pool fringed with seaweed, large enough comfortably to accommodate one person, or two if they are reasonably well acquainted.

The massive, 200ft (61m) pyramid of L'Etac de Sercq (formerly L'Etat or Le Tas) looms $^1/_2$ mile to the south, about a furlong in length and half that breadth; a string of half-tide rocks (*demies*) and Pierre du Cours are the vestiges of its former link with Sark. Semi-detached to the north is pierced Quête d'Amont, a smaller pyramid used as a fisherman's mark, and north-west are Les Vingt Clos, a chain of submerged rocks. As only five among them are charted, perhaps it should be 'Cinq' Clos.

L'Etac's razor-backed ridge is flanked by steep slopes covered with soft, rich thrift and ideal for the puffins that nest in its honeycomb of burrows. Some years ago Jersey naturalists Dick and Frances Le Sueur found a pair of storm petrels nesting there and, in 1957, Guy Messenger, master of botany at Uppingham School, identified twenty-two species of flowering plants on an April visit.

Port Gorey to Les Fontaines

Sark's southern limits have offshore rocks of all sizes, from the islets of Moie du Viet (formerly Bretagne Uset), Sercul, Grande Bretagne (formerly Moie de Port Gorey) and Moie à Charbon to the dwarf menaces of Les Coffres (Coffins) and Petite Baveuse (little slobberer). A succession of small bays and gullies—Brenière, Clouet, Plat Rué and La Louge among them—lead to the deep inlet of Port Gorey (or Goury), where mining equipment used to be landed and silver ore loaded on schooners, cutters and barges. A path from the old landing and its rusted mooring rings ascends through the ruined engine-house, past two ventilation shafts to the tiny hamlet of Little Sark, once a bustling industrial centre. A notice warns of open mineshafts concealed in dense undergrowth.

Dangers seaward, too; yachting writer Adlard Coles says: 'from Les Hautes Boues to L'Etac should not be attempted without local knowledge on board'. The coastline turns north into Rouge Câne (or Caneau) bay, with Blakemore's Bath at its southern end. The little rock pool was a favourite of Galway-born poet Trevor Blakemore, who died in 1953, soon after a last visit to his '. . . quiet isle of crags and rocks and tides, guarded remote from man . . .' which he first saw as a youth of seventeen in 1898 and where he contentedly spent much of his adult life.

Les Coursiers, a channel that dries on low springs to provide good catches of ormers, flows between Moie de la Bretagne and Le Coursier rock off the headland north of Rouge Câne. Le Coursier has five rock pools—the deepest, largest and possibly Sark's most beautiful being Adonis; more irregular in shape than Venus, it has a shimmering fringe of delicate, multi-coloured seaweeds. It can be reached only one hour each side of low water from Little Sark, is easily missed and, like all the rock scrambles, should never be attempted alone. A fall could leave you at the mercy of water that rises very fast and has a savage undertow.

Les Fontaines bay just to the north takes its name from a stream that rises halfway up the easy cliff path and is not to be confused with Les Fontaines south-east of l'Eperquerie. Craggy Moie de la Fontaine and a high reef almost landlock the little bay, the sea reaching it through a creek that offers superb swimming. A rock near the Moie remarkably resembles Queen Victoria's head; another 'bust' of the monarch is at the tip of Pointe Derrible.

Vermandaie and Grande Grève

It is possible to scramble on to Vermandaie (or Vermandaye, Vermandée, Vermandez) and Grande Grève bays; but low water is needed to get through the arch in Pointe le Jeu (or Joue). Make sure of the tide; the climb from Vermandaie is tricky since the path disappeared under a landslide. South of Vermandaie, whitened by generations of shags, is the deep gully of Creux Blanc, with the black hole of Creux Noir opening from it, and the sea gurgling over La Baveuse offshore.

La Grande Grève's broad expanse of firm sand contracts at high water to a patch of shingle at the foot of the path and steps leading down from the north end of La Coupée. A pleasanter descent to the south has disappeared under an impenetrable tangle of brambles and bracken, as has the well-loved walk to Vermandaie from just beyond La Coupée.

Arched La Chapelle, La Pierre Ormers and spiky Les Epines are all in Grande Grève, with Boue de la Baie 3ft under low water on the western approach. Caves and secluded coves; winkles for easy picking; carnelians and other semi-precious stones discernible among myriad shells by the sharp-sighted; splendid bathing—Grande Grève has them all, but don't get caught, like the hero and heroine of John Oxenham's *Pearl of Pearl Island,* in the current that sweeps round Pointe le Jeu.

Port és Saies to Havre Gosselin

Sandy Port és Saies (or Sées) to the north can be reached only by boat, or by scrambling at low tide past Creux Gardin chimney, since the path below Dosdâne cottages collapsed in a landslip, unless you climb hand-over-hand down a wire cable. In the far corner of the bay, shored by pit props and running wet from a subterranean stream, is a shaft reputed to have a clifftop exit near Dixcart Lane—perhaps a ventilator for old mine workings.

Cliffs dropping straight into deep water prevent scrambling from Port és Saies past Moie des Orgeries, round Longue Pointe, and through the line of rocks that terminate seaward in pierced Pierre du Norman, to Le Havre Gosselin. A fierce undertow has claimed the lives of several swimmers and the only safe way to view this coast, with its caves of Heaven, Hell and high-vaulted Victor Hugo, is by dinghy.

Railings on the left of the steep path from Pilcher Monument to Havre Gosselin and its little jetty guard a sheer drop known as Creux à Jean Drillot. In 1887 Drillot and two companions landed in pitch darkness on the overhanging iron ladder near the present jetty. The others went ahead and, on reaching the clifftop, called to Drillot; there was no reply. He had plunged to his death in the sea.

Philippe de Carteret, a fisherman descendant of the first seigneur, once lived—according to Louisa Lane's *Sark Legends* — above Havre Gosselin. He turned smuggler and one day his son Helier found him carousing with companions in a cave. They argued and Philippe knocked Helier from his boat. His body was never found and the broken-hearted father died soon afterwards.

In Havre Gosselin is the deep conger hole of Houle Genette. The anchorage is protected from north, east and south, but when there is a warning of south-westerly gales yachtsmen weigh anchor.

Gouliot headland to Moie de Mouton

Geologist Dr G. H. Plymen considered that Sark's 'most picturesque scenery is . . . west of Havre Gosselin, where the isolated islands of hornblende schist show various stages in the process of total destruction'. This is the coast beyond rocky Telegraph Bay, where majestic cliffs below the grazing of Côtil Martin culminate in Gouliot headland. A telephone cable dips across a narrow gap to the great, green mass of Moie du Gouliot (known by old fishermen as Moie au Sieur Peter), then in a longer arc over the 80yd (73m) of Gouliot Passage to the heights of Brecqhou. The tide rips through at more than 8 mph and hurricane-force winds can atomise the water to clifftop height in a huge screen of white spray.

Below the headland, down a path alarmingly fringing the gaping Creux à Mèche, are the Gouliot caves, with their famed inner complex (see p 71). From the top there is a fine view of Sark's coast northward and across l'Eperquerie common to Alderney, with a clear day picking out Burhou, Ortac and Les Casquets. The path north loops inland to avoid a plunge down unprotected Saut à Juan (formerly Saujouin). Said to have been inspired by a romantic lover's leap (John's Jump), the name more probably derives from *sans jaon* (without gorse). A fork doubles back to a small quarry and the other side of this sheer drop. Ahead to the left a new *creux*, already 10ft (3m) deep, appears to be forming and, as the path turns back to Beauregard, a crumbling dry-stone wall drops steeply down the now overgrown *côtil* to a gap 30ft (9m) wide and several times that depth. On the other side is Grosse Moie de Mouton; in living memory this was reached by a flimsy wooden bridge, across which sheep were driven to graze when the Sarkese used all available agricultural land.

This massive outcrop and its smaller neighbour, Petit Moie de Mouton, are accessible at sea level by scrambling from Port à la Jument. For half-an-hour each side of low springs you can explore the lofty cavern that pierces the bigger *moie;* at other times a dinghy can get in from the south, where Creux à Bénarde rends open the shoreward cliffs.

Port à la Jument to Saignie

A cliff path from Le Vieux Port farmhouse zigzags down the promontory that divides Port à la Jument bay. There is little use now for the bay's seaweed hoist; the *vraic* pronounced 'wrack', once the farmers' natural source of fertilizer, has been largely supplanted by chemicals.

Passing Terre au Sieur headland and several deep gullies, the low-water scrambler reaches a boulder-strewn bay, Pégâne. The word, of Celtic derivation, means 'rocks connected together, or through which it is difficult to pass', according to nineteenth-century Guernsey etymologist, the Rev R.H. Tourtel. The scrambler would hardly disagree!

From Pégâne a gap between the rock mass of Tintageu and a high headland leads to Port du Moulin. Tintageu, also Celtic, means 'rocks placed or lying on one another', presumably also the origin of Tintagel in Cornwall.

A branch from the main path up the cliff crosses La Petite Coupée to the head opposite Tintageu. Beside the main path is the platform of the ancient monastic watermill, with a little waterfall still tumbling just above it. Higher, near L'Ecluse holiday apartments, a long, deep hollow, now dry, was one of three reservoirs built by the monks.

Port du Moulin is a particularly pleasant bay. Inshore is Moie de Telle, offshore Platte rock and the underwater shoals of Petite Banquette and Les Epiceresses. Beyond a graceful arch flooded at high water stand Les Autelets (altars), easily reached across the rocks at low tide—Grand Autelet, riven in two with some vegetation on the square, larger section; Blanc (or Petit) Autelet, whitened by generations of seabirds, and l'Epile (needle). These impressive stacks and their nesting ledges can be viewed from above by following the cliff path, as can neighbouring Saignie Bay.

Accessible by scrambling on from Les Autelets at low water, semi-circular, red-cliffed Saignie Bay has another fine arch and five caves—including one pillared like a Gothic church, and a souffleur that works in north-west winds.

La Foureuse to Le Bec du Nez

Beyond Saignie a succession of rocky headlands, gullies and islets challenge the scrambler: La Foureuse, pierced by a branching cave; the high cliffs of Banque à la Vielle and the hollow of Le Vané; Moie à Chats (Moie Cat in patois); le Chameau, topped by its camel's head; a rock in the likeness of Napoleon Buonaparte and Les Sept Moies. When you finally draw level with Guillaumesse, drying 20ft (6m) high some 40yd (36.5m) offshore, the black platform of Le Platon is just ahead, a splendid base for mullet fishing when the wind is easterly, with a fairly easy climb to L'Eperquerie common.

On the common are the butts and parade ground of the old militia; the little guardhouse above the landing became a cottage which, incredibly, housed a family of ten up to World War II, but is now in ruins.

North of Le Platon two great chasms are separated by the cliffs of La Pêche Colin. From the top of the second a path drops steeply, then forks upwards and right to the chimney entrance of Les Boutiques caves; these were perhaps once used at this only high and dry section as a warehouse for smuggled goods — their role in John Oxenham's *Carette of Sark.*

The most northerly of four sea entrances is at the end of a long, vaulted tunnel just west of Le Pertu, the gap at the end of mainland Sark, where it is easy to climb down the cliff. Woolnough's 1861 description of Les Boutiques is as good as any since: 'The depressing effect of the gloom is heightened by the silence, sometimes broken by the distant rush of imprisoned waters . . . two arched mouths run out to sea, the floor covered with shallow seaweed ponds. The roof drips with water, and at the sea entry are clusters of bright ferns overhead, in beautiful contrast with the reddish-brown of the quartz-veined rock.'

Unlike Les Gouliots, however, the walls inside are devoid of marine life, despite the sea covering them at high water. Near the north entrance is the secluded platform of La Bertaude, ideal for unobserved sunbathing, if you can find it.

Sark ends in three rock piles of descending height: grassy La Grune, separated at high water by Le Pertu, through which a fishing boat can just pass; Corbée (or Courbée) du Nez, hooked like the bridge of a monstrous nose, and Bec du Nez, usually called The Point. Le Bec's highwater part is known in patois as Grune à Pie Marange (oystercatcher's rock). Standing sentinel to the west are Les Trois Grunes; to the east lie underwater Sardrière, the drying rocks of Moulinet and Jolicot, and the brooding mass of La Pêcheresse.

L'Eperquerie to Banquette landing

The way turns south past the fisherman's outcrop of Congriére and along the cliffs of La Charrière Brâton to the old landing place, where cargo was sometimes unloaded before World War II, but it is now used only by small boats. A wide path ascends through an ancient, high stone wall, probably once the door or *lû* that gave its name to little Baie Sous Lû below. There are three old cannon on L'Eperquerie, one broken in two to serve as mooring posts.

South of the landing are another detached Moie de Telle, then the twin tongues of Pignon and Pointe Bruge leading to Les Fontaines bay of Great Sark, through two arched rocks known as the Twin Sisters or Fairy Grotto, the latter name given by Toplis, who also painted the pretty Fern (or Grass) Cave south of steps from the path above. Another cave leads to Creux Bélêts chimney, 120ft (36.5m) deep, and above high water, so the sea cannot wash away its fallen soil and rocks.

Past Le Saleux outcrop is the huge chasm of Grand Creux, L-shaped like a Wellington boot, and the Red (or Drinking Horse) Cave, its central pillar formation suggesting a horse lowering its head to drink the inrushing tide.

Off Pointe de l'Huitrière with its Creux à Caux (limehole) is L'Huitrière (oyster) rock; further out lie underwater Boue Guernesiaise (another rock by the same name is west of L'Etac); the 10ft (3m) squarish Noire Pierre and, awash at low water, La Pavlaison. Some rarely visited gullies, offering perfect bathing at half-tide up, end in Banquette landing's platform and an easy climb to Le Fort. Confusingly, Banquette *Bay* is the west-coast sweep from Brecqhou to Le Bec.

Grève de la Ville and La Maseline

An overgrown, well-concealed goat path links the ascents from Banquette and Grève de la Ville, but it is easier to view Creux à Chiens gully and the heights of La Quarée, Le Roqui and Grève Michelle from the sea. A lovely, fern-lined path, yellow with primroses in spring, winds down from the clifftop to Grève de la Ville. Out to sea stand the fairyland crags of Petite Moie, 56ft (17m) high, with Le Bec at its northern end, as on Sark itself, and La Gorge at the south. At the far end of the bay is the arched Chapelle és Mauves (gulls' chapel) rock and the loose-surfaced earth mound of Moie Navets. A tunnel opening halfway up Navets contains 'a Fat Man's Misery', notes Latrobe, 'a small cave in which the larger members of a party are inserted to see if they are able to emerge through a hole in the top . . .'

High in rocks on the left of the tunnel exit is Mercury's Pool. Fast scramblers can continue at low springs through Les Abîmes, a series of small caves and gullies below Pointe Robert lighthouse, past the fang of La Rai (skate) and Le Bedan Robert to Sark's third Creux à Chien, the 30yd-long Dog Cave, which barks loudly when tide and wind decree. A channel 150yd (137m) wide and 20ft (6m) deep separates Pointe Robert from La Grande Moie; greener at its 90ft (27m) summit than Petite Moie, but equally enchantingly Aegean, it has Le Parquet as its northern flank and Le Piquillon at the south.

Ahead is Maseline bay and harbour. To explore the intervening coast–Bas Crévé, La Valette bay, Moie Richard and La Porte Toussaint–a boat is needed, as also for the deep cave in Pointe Cagnons, behind the telephone box on the south spur of Maseline jetty. Founiais (or Founet) rock and its *boue* are just north-east of the harbour, with Grand and Petit Huart a little further out and a moaning buoy $2^1/_4$ miles east marking Blanchard, which shows only on low springs. Through Cagnons tunnel is La Chaussée Chenchannée, the inlet at the foot of Harbour Hill, and the end of the forty-two mile coastal circuit.

It can be made by boat. George Guille, who offers visitors this opportunity in summer, says, 'There have been some unwelcome changes in Sark, but its magic is still the same as ever as we go round the bottom.'

SARK

Visiting yachtsmen have a choice of anchorages, among them Grève de la Ville; inside Maseline jetty; off Creux Harbour or inside above half-tide; Dixcart and Derrible bays, all on the east coast; Havre Gosselin and Grande Grève on the west. Directions are given in *Channel Pilot* (vol 2) and *Channel Harbours and Anchorages* (K. Adlard Coles).

In an island so totally dependent on shipping and tourism, it is surprising that a harbour master was first appointed as recently as 1979. His 1991 salary is £1,316, with the cost of harbour repairs estimated at £15,000.

4   THE WAY OF LIFE

'Take the best and leave the worst'
'Sally Water', children's song

MANY of Sark's distinctive customs and traditions have fallen victim to twentieth-century influences, though others survive. The island costume—black peasant bonnet and long dress, with purple shawl, now the treasured heirloom of a few old ladies—is worn only at special request, as also are the brilliant scarlet tunics of the Royal Sark Militia.

Almost a memory now is *la joncquière,* or 'green bed', stuffed with fresh straw, though its wooden frame may still be found in one or two cottages. Also half-forgotten is *La Veille* (or *Longue Veille*), a revel current when knitting was the popular home industry. Groups of islanders, who gathered to work late into the night, were visited by a man in a white sheet, holding up a horse's or donkey's head on a stick. He went from house to house, cabaret to cabaret (as the bars were called) chasing people and trying to bite them with the animal's jaws, which he snapped open and shut by means of cords from inside his shroud. Following him came a boisterous crowd of onlookers and, Cachemaille noted, 'much time was wasted, bad habits were contracted and were followed by immorality'.

SARK

On La Fête de Saint-Jean, Midsummer's Day, horses were garlanded and young people paired off to ride them two up; every house was open to them and tables were laden with plum cake, yeast buns, locally brewed cider and spider crabs, which fishermen had brought up by the sackful. On the common above Les Lâches the youngsters danced round singing:

> Sally, Sally Water, sprinkle in the pan,
> Take a young lady before a young man,
> Take the best and leave the worst
> And take the one that you love best.
> Now you're married I wish you joy,
> The First of May, the Second of June
> And kiss away . . .

on which they would disappear in couples behind the decent seclusion of broom and gorse.

Dances and songs

Traditional dances included 'La Frigande', with intricate footwork on a chalked cross; 'Danse de la Brouaise', with a broomstick; 'Danse de Chapieux', with hats on the floor. At the end of communal ploughing, when the huge farm implement was drawn by six draught horses, and women carried yeast cakes and steaming jugs of coffee to refresh the workers, came the festival of La Grande Tierrue, with singing and dancing far into the night.

Sark's songs were ususally local variations of those sung in the other islands, French or Norman French in origin, handed down orally from generation to generation, often genially bawdy and down-to-earth in sentiment, sometimes slightly macabre. A typical example is 'Man Buonhomme est bein Malade':

50

Man mari est bein malade
Et j'n'sais qu'est'ce qu'i a

J'm'en fus-t-en Guer-ne-si
Du lundi à mercredi

Mais quan j'ervins i'tait mort
Et encore ensev'li

J'appis mes p'tites ciselettes
Point à point j'l'décousais

Mais quan j'appraichis p'tite gorgette
J'craignais qu'i n'me mordisse

J'l'appis par l'gros orté
J'l'env'yis avau l'côti

J'priyis tous les corbins
D'v'ni prieu auprès d'li

(My husband's very ill, with what I do not know. I went to Guernsey from Monday till Wednesday and when I came back I found him dead, all ready to be laid out. I took my small scissors and stitched him up step by step, until I came to his little throat. Then I was afraid he'd bite me, so I took him by the big toe and threw him over the cliff. I begged the crows to come and pray by him.)

Other old favourites included 'La Madeleine', 'L'bon Marain', 'J'ai Perdu ma Faumme', 'Belle Rose', 'Les Trois Demoiselles et le Cordonnier', 'Les Troies Jaunnes Tambours', 'Marguerite', 'L'p'tit Couturier', 'L'Vingt-Cinquième du mois d'Octobre'. Among those brought back from France in World War I were 'Alouette', 'Auprès de ma

Blonde' and—sung with appropriate gestures—on the old sickness theme:

> Madame Le Gallez est bien malade,
> La pouce comme çi, la pouce comme ça,
> L'oeil fermé, la bouche tournée,
> Et la tête qui livre et les pieds aussi . . .

(Mme Le Gallez is very poorly, the thumb like this, the thumb like that, closed eye, twisted mouth, the head hanging loose and the feet, too)

Thanks to such traditionalists as Phyllis Le Feuvre, Henry Carré and Hilary Carré, the songs and dances have so far survived.

Festivals

Other traditions persist, too, like that of Good Friday, when boys sail model boats on Beauregard duckpond.

The Wesleyan chapel has an unusually large congregation on Primrose Sunday, often the second in April, but with no fixed date, as it depends on a Methodist roadman's assessment of when Sark's primroses are at their best. Children bring freshly picked bunches to be received at the chapel and sent to Guernsey hospitals.

In July comes the cattle show; in August the garden and agricultural produce show, and in September the horse show, featuring the Sark Derby, with mounted draught horses thundering round Clos de Milieu.

During the week before Christmas carol singers carry their lanterns from house to house, reverent voices progressively lubricated by open-door hospitality. The money they collect helps support the Flying Christine and various local charities while another Christmas collection shows the islanders' gratitude to the crews of the Shipping Company's boats for ensuring their supplies and link with

Guernsey in all weathers. The first drink in the taverns on Christmas morning is always 'on the house' and with Sark friends there is potent home-made sloe gin and gorse-flower wine to be sampled. Water in the wells is said to turn to wine on Christmas Eve, but anyone drinking it will hear a voice prophesying his death before the year's end.

Communal activities

The sense of community is still strong. After weddings the bride and groom tour the island in a carriage, taking cake and wine to friends prevented by age or illness from attending the reception.

News of a death and funeral arrangements comes from *les avertisseurs,* persons—often nephews of the deceased—sent to inform relatives, friends and neighbours. The coffin is usually carried to church by nephews of the deceased, and escorted by immediate family. The coffins come from Guernsey; the son of a former *prévôt,* who acts as undertaker, always keeps a couple in reserve as insurance against Sark being cut off by gales.

Former religious hatreds are forgotten. The score of Roman Catholics, lacking their own place of worship since they lost the White Chapel near La Forge, celebrate Mass on Mondays in the Island Hall and once accepted an invitation to use the Methodist church. Remembrance Sunday is interdenominational, with the Methodists sharing a morning service at the Anglican church and the Anglicans going to chapel in the evening. Sark's British Legion branch, 25 in number, parades for morning service on Remembrance Sunday, as does the dozen-strong Loyalty Lodge of the Royal Antediluvian Order of Buffaloes, which had its Diamond Jubilee in 1981.

There are food parcels at Christmas for the old folk, donated and distributed by the 'Buffs' and by the Why Not League, a women's group formed in the 1920s, which gives money to the thirty or so over-seventies on birthdays and at

Easter, raising it by jumble sales and collections. There are gifts, too, for those in hospital. Benevolent work is also done by the British Legion and by the two dozen ladies of the Methodist Women's Fellowship, who hold weekly meetings and organise two annual sales of work for such causes as the marine ambulance, Red Cross or chapel restoration.

SPORT AND RECREATION

Outdoor sports facilities are limited. Up to and even during World War II there was cricket, football, netball and hockey, also an active boxing and physical training class until the Germans stopped it, presumably fearing the emergence of a local maquis. Soccer matches against visiting Guernsey teams are played occasionally, but more popular currently are the clay pigeon and sporting rifle clubs, one of whose members represented Guernsey in the 1978 and 1982 Commonwealth Games. Tennis courts and a riding school are recent acquisitions.

Indoors there is badminton at the Hall, but the keenest rivalry is in darts and shove-ha'penny tournaments at the Bel Air and Mermaid taverns. There are whist drives, dances and, in summer, a weekly film show at the Hall.

Sark Theatre Group stages an annual production of surprisingly high standard, there is an enterprising youth theatre group and the Music Society holds recitals of chamber music, though these, like cocktail and bridge parties, are mainly attended by the immigrants. Sunday is maintained as a day of rest and the bars are closed.

NAMES AND NICKNAMES

The Sarkese can be recognised by their family names: Baker, Carré, de Carteret, Falle, Guille, Hamon, Le Feuvre, Perrée and Vibert. The most popular Christian names are English: Frank, Frederick, George, Philip, John, James and William.

Nicknames are common, though rarely bestowed on immigrants. Among recent examples are L'Berger, L'Corbin, L'Patron, Gros Fred, Majohn, Johnny Lobster, Johnny Crow, Johnny Snooks, Jack Dads, Hero, The Goat, The Zebra, Billy Fish, Fifty-fifty, Christmas, Squeaker, Pegleg, The Chocolate Soldier, King Kong, Captain Pugwash, Bang-Bang, Jumbo, Plop, Flash, Black Hannah and Pretty Polly. Les Lapins (the rabbits) or les Corbins (the Crows) are terms applied generally to the Sarkese by other Channel Islanders; a Guernseyman is known as l'âne (donkey), a Jerseyman as l'crapaud (toad).

LOCAL DISHES

Before World War I baking was still by wall oven *(l'trepi),* often fired by furze roots. Farmers having a cow or pig killed by the island butcher would take house-to-house orders for cuts; and the stone cider-press at Petit Dixcart was turned by a horse to produce the traditional Sark beverage.

A favourite dish was *Sark Dinner,* a version of pot-au-feu; it is still eaten, though less popular. The ingredients are a joint of pork (sometimes the trotters), parsnips, onions, turnips, carrots, potatoes, suet dough, egg, milk, currants and seasoning. The pork and vegetables are cooked in a big earthenware jar; a 'spotted dick' pudding made with dough, currants, egg and a little milk, is added and, half-an-hour before serving, the potatoes go in, too.

Conger soup is still highly rated. The head and tail of the big sea eel are simmered for $1\frac{1}{2}$ hours with potatoes and other root vegetables. Shredded spring cabbage, peas, marigold leaves, bouquet garni and a generous slice of butter are added to the strained stock and this is returned to the heat until the vegetables are cooked. Milk and seasoning are added and, on serving, the soup is sprinkled with marigold petals.

Conger can be stuffed and baked, or steamed. Local sand eels are excellent dipped in flour or batter and fried; while ormers make a succulent casserole and are also delicious in pickle, or beaten flat and fried like a veal escalope. Sark lobsters and chancre or spider crabs are other prized specialities.

A DYING LANGUAGE

The local patois, Sark French or Sercqais, is sadly dying out owing to immigration, improved communications and tourism. Still spoken by the older Sarkese and a few of the younger generation, it is heard far less than immediately after World War II. Sixty years ago the patois was almost universal; the islanders who were then children speak English today with some hesitation, thinking in patois, before translating into what is to them still a foreign tongue.

Sercqais is derived from the Norman French brought from Jersey by sixteenth-century settlers. Never written down, but passed on from generation to generation, it was preserved for hundreds of years in almost virgin purity, thanks to Sark's relative isolation and despite the more orthodox French spoken in church, school and court.

It has marked differences from Jersiais and Guernesiais, and the Alderney French lost for ever with that island's evacuation during World War II. Prince Lucien Bonaparte, a nineteenth-century philologist, considered Sercqais the purest and best language of the Channel Islands.

Many words are unique to Sark, such as *terriôt* for muckcart; the Jersey equivalent is *hernet*. Clipped pronunciation reduces the French *je suis* to *j'sis; il sera* to *i'sa*. The masculine article *le* is never given full value, always shortened to *l'*. Some recently introduced words, obviously of English origin (eg *frôc* for dress) have been given a Gallic flavour, but where the French would address you as *mon cher* (my dear) or *mon vieux* (old chap), the Sarkese say *man pôvre ami* (my poor friend).

Guernsey and Jersey have dictionaries of their patois, but, apart from a short and partly inaccurate glossary in *The Guernsey Magazine* (December 1875), there appears to be no written Sercqais. Even at that time Cachemaille commented: '. . . Sark patois is undergoing changes and gradually becoming extinct. The children do not now pronounce it so well nor so clippingly nor with that seemingly careful and sharp sounding of every vowel and consonant to be noticed in the speech of the older generation.'

The present older generation mostly believe the patois will have virtually disappeared in twenty years' time, though even a few months before her death in 1974 Dame Sibyl was more optimistic. She learned Sercqais from her nanny, believed it showed Scandinavian influences and held that the natural inquisitiveness of children, hearing their parents talk patois, would enable the language to survive. Michael Beaumont, her grandson and successor as seigneur, does not speak it, however.

It would be a sin of philological omission to let Sercqais die without record (see Appendix D).

WITCHES AND GHOSTS

Many once-prevalent superstitions also seem to be slowly disappearing. The old farm and cottage chimneys have ledges called witches' seats, reputedly resting places to placate the casters of spells on their nocturnal flights. The prosaic explanation is that they were to prevent rain water seeping under the formerly thatched roofs. But houses built since thatch disappeared have the ledges—and Sark certainly had its witches.

Jean Nicolle, tenant of La Sablonnerie, when found guilty of sorcery at a Guernsey trial in 1620, was whipped, had an ear cut off and suffered lifelong banishment. His wife, Rachel Alexandre, was burned alive seven years later, and three other Nicolles from Sark were tried for practising the black arts: Job, banished in 1627; Jehan, set at liberty, and Nathan, no verdict recorded, both in 1631.

Within living memory Dame Sibyl's second daughter, Douce, had her warts charmed away by a 'wise-man', while a sick cow at La Seigneurie was apparently cured by a magic length of white wool tied round her hock. Less pleasantly, there are tales of children infested with lice, as a result of spells cast as punishment for their parents.

Since television arrived, there are fewer ghost stories such as that of Tchi-co, the phantom black dog of the dead, also known in Guernsey as part of a devil-worship cult . . . of coffins crossing La Coupée at night . . . of hooded monks and a headless rider on a white horse. . . of cattle kneeling in adoration on the Eve of St John.

During the 1870s an English couple, the man an artist, were living in Sark—a less respectful version says the girl was cohabiting with two artists. Many years after her death, the parish nurse claimed, on her own deathbed, to have seen strangulation marks on the girl's throat. A cross staked into her grave was repeatedly found lying on its side. Finally the cross was removed, but her ghost reputedly continued to haunt Dixcart Valley.

Another spectral lady was said to walk down the stairs at La Jaspellerie and ride a horse on the lawn outside. An English-woman on holiday at the same house woke early one morning to hear male voices chanting; she roused her husband, who could hear nothing. Some years later, at a Catholic mass in Southern France, she heard the same music, sung by monks who told her it was an ancient Norman chant–perhaps an echo of Sark's sixth-century monastery.

The ghosts are probably tricks of light and mist, their sounds produced by the wailing wind and soughing sea, but there is a strangely haunting, though never unwelcoming atmosphere in parts of the island, especially on Little Sark. It is easy to understand why poet Trevor Blakemore, echoing Swinburne, so fervently believed in Sark's

'Elementals', the title of one of his books. And a Jersey legend says the sound of crying, heard on nights when the wind is making for a storm, comes from five weeping children of Sark's colonists, drowned in 1631 when their boat shattered on the Pierres de Lecq and fifteen lives were lost. They call it *le cri de la mer.*

SHIPWRECKS

Wrecks and drownings have been recurring themes in the Sark story. Paulus Warnefridi recorded the wreck of three French vessels off Evoda (probably Givaude) *c* AD 780. Early evidence is otherwise scanty, apart from an unnamed boat sinking near Sark in 1608. In 1779, the East Indiaman *Valentine* struck Le Nesté and sank with her cargo of spices, dyewood, gold dust and brocade. The crew reached Brecqhou and a century later rich brocade still graced many humble Sark cottages. In 1974, a French diver claimed to have located the *Valentine,* some of her guns being still intact. An unnamed prize-of-war, captured near St Helena and said to be a whaler, also sank near Sark on the night the *Valentine* went down.

Another unnamed ship was lost off Sark in 1816. Twenty years later, Professor White of London University, with his wife, mother and two Guernsey pilots, were drowned after leaving Sark for St Peter Port in an open boat. Three more Guernseymen were lost and one saved in 1843, when the fishing boat *Elizabeth* was rammed off Sark by a marauding French *chasse-marée, l'Evangelique*

In 1847 the cutter *Lady of Sark*, built earlier that year in Guernsey, was struck by lightning and foundered in Creux Harbour; she was subsequently raised but became a total wreck when torn from her moorings nine years later. The *Ellen* went down east of Sark in 1853.

A postscript to Woolnough's *Scrambles in Sark*, published in 1861, tells of a dramatic rescue on 19 February in that year from the Sark cutter *Rival* when she broke in two outside Creux Harbour, after missing her moorings in a gale: 'The crew and passengers were saved, owing chiefly, under God, to the energy and courage of Philippe Le Feuvre, a young Sarkese of La Ville. He, while others on the harbour above hung back, offered to go alone to the rock on which they had taken refuge. Joined by three onlookers, they together brought off four men and two women, who for six hours had hardly kept their foothold against the wave.' Two seamen had escaped in the dinghy being towed astern of the cutter and this was taken over by Le Feuvre. On his first trip the terrified women would not let go of the rock and clamber down to him, so he had to return, climb up and carry them to the boat. His bravery was rewarded by a testimonial fund in Guernsey.

Those were grim years: 1862, French cutter *Alcyane* lost north-east of Sark; 1863, *Les Douze Apôtres* sank at Havre Gosselin, her skipper subsequently given permission to sell off what could be salvaged of her cargo; 1870, Guernsey brig *Elizabeth* wrecked on the Humps, her crew landed in Sark; 1885, French dandy *Charles* on Grune au Nord; 1887, Guernsey brig *Joseph & Margaret* on Blanchard; 1888, sloop *Holbeach* on Grune au Nord.

In March 1895 six men of Sark set off in the seven-ton *Vigilant*, built on the island thirty years earlier, to gather vraic from Herm. Turning for home the boat struck a rock, holed and sank. Skipper Carré and his five companions sought refuge on Godin and were rescued two days later when Captain Bichard, taking the *Assistance* on its bi-weekly cargo trip to Sark, was told, by frenzied relatives, of their disappearance.

Two boats called *Courier*, both built in Southampton, plied between Guernsey, Alderney and Sark. They were known locally as the 'Big' and 'Little' Couriers and the latter, launched in 1876, had a relatively uneventful career until sold to a Greek firm in 1913. The 'Big' *Courier*, 130ft

($39^1/_2$m) long and launched in 1883, was to earn great renown in the islands for her all-weather sailings under Captain Whales. There was tragedy, too.

She struck a rock off Jethou in 1901, was beached on Crevichon and eventually salvaged. In April 1906, with Seigneur Collings and his wife aboard, she again hit a rock off Jethou and sank in seven fathoms. Attempts to launch the two lifeboats failed. Ten on board were drowned. The rest escaped, fourteen of them landed by a small dinghy on La Grosse Ferrière rock, to be rescued by the steam tug *Alert*. Collings and his wife were among those picked up; desperately ill, she was on her way to see a London specialist and died a few months later.

The *Courier's* skipper was found guilty of negligence at the subsequent inquiry. Again salvaged, the *Courier* was still on the inter-island run when World War II started. A surprised resident from Little Sark found her ferrying American troops on the Clyde during the war; she afterwards made a triumphant return to the islands, but proved too expensive to run and was scrapped in Holland during 1951.

Three years before the 1906 disaster, John William Falle and his son William Slowley Falle of Beauregard were drowned 'durant la traversée de Guernesey à Sercq', as a memorial tablet records in St Peter's Church. The bodies were never found, but their portraits still hang at Beauregard.

One of the last ships to leave Guernsey on the traditional route to South America was the barquentine *Geraldine* in 1916. Howling south-westerly gales in the Bay of Biscay drove her steadily back for six days, until the London trader *Channel Queen* got her in tow east of Sark. She sank a few miles from the haven of St Peter Port. In the following year the French steamer *Hirondelle* went down in 170ft (52m) of water south of Sark. Another French ship, *Jeanne Marie*, carrying copper and zinc ingots, was lost off Sark in 1918; thirteen years later the Italian salvage vessel *Raffio* turned turtle with the loss of one life while trying to raise the valuable cargo.

Inter-war wrecks in Sark waters included the steamer *Cairnside* (1922), ketch *Charles Emile* (1925), French schooner *Le Tourmente* (1927), French ketches *Membraze* (1930) and *Le Poilu* (1932), and the motor vessel *Joybell II* (1933). There have since been no major wrecks around Sark, perhaps owing to fewer cross-Channel vessels trading with Jersey, but many smaller boats and some lives have been lost, notably those of John Hamon and Willie Remphrey in 1946, when their punt capsized off Les Lâches.

In 1982, the Isle of Sark Shipping Company sold the *Ile de Serk* to a company trading in the Caribbean. She sailed across the Atlantic to continue her working life, remembered with affection by the islanders and countless visitors. Then, in 1990, her life ended when a hurricane left her high and dry on the beach of Dominica, where she was photographed by a Sark resident on sailing holiday in the West Indies.

A Sark law forbids shooting seagulls and taking their eggs, though the latter ban is often broken. The cries of these birds can warn boatmen of rocks hidden by the swirling mists that so often and suddenly shroud the island waters.

5   LIVING ON THE ROCKS

'In the shadows between great cliffs
And granite stacks is the home of the birds'.
                              Trevor Blakemore

COUNTING THE BIRDS

FROM the first approach to Sark with gulls shrieking overhead to the later discovery of countless tiny wrens on the tableland, you are always aware of the birds, strangely tame and, on closer acquaintance, ready to eat out of your hand.

Systematic research into the bird life began in 1966, when a public meeting elected the Sark Ornithological Committee to prepare a full list of species 'authentically identified'. While studying the island's history and geology, to determine its changing habitat for birds, they found there had been great numbers of wildfowl, such as Mallard and Teal, during the seventeenth and eighteenth centuries, in contrast to the rare duck that now seeks shelter. It suggested there was far more standing fresh water, clearly visible from the air, at a time when virtually the only trees were in the cider-apple orchards.

As a starting point the committee took the list of ninety-eight Sark species in Roderick Dobson's *The Birds of the Channel Islands* (1952). His summary of authentic data, scattered through literature and in private papers and diaries, was all eventually verified by new sightings. The process speeded up in 1970 when committee member

Philip J. Guille started to net and ring, licensed by the Channel Islands Bird Ringing Scheme. Thanks to the nets on wooded, marshy ground below his secluded house on the north-east coast, some hitherto unsuspected visitors have been discovered and fresh data provided on migratory patterns — for example, by the Swallow ringed in Sark on 20 September 1972 and recovered three months later near Durban, Natal. All recoveries in the reverse direction of swallows ringed in Durban appear to have been in the USSR, eastwards from the Ukraine, while West European and British recoveries had all been ringed in Transvaal, Cape Province and Kimberley Station, never in Natal.

In November 1971 Guille netted a Great Tit ringed six weeks earlier in Latvia, 1,087 miles (1,700km) from Sark. This and other findings such as a Snipe ringed in Denmark and picked up dead in a Sark field, and the first Channel Island recording of a Lesser Spotted Woodpecker, a continental bird probably from Scandinavia, revised the supposition that most passage migrants in Sark were en route either to or from England. Some from Scandinavia evidently travel across the Baltic and Low Countries, before wheeling south over France.

The 169 species recorded in 1966-74 are in breeding and non-breeding categories, the latter far more numerous. Breeding residents include the Wren, 150 of which were ringed in 1973; among the common species, it compensates for high mortality by prolific breeding.

The thirty-three established resident breeders are: Shag, Mallard, Kestrel, Pheasant, Oystercatcher, Great Black-backed Gull, Herring Gull, Woodpigeon, Collared Dove, Skylark, Raven, Carrion Crow, Magpie, Great Tit, Blue Tit, Short-toed Treecreeper, Wren, Missel Thrush, Song Thrush, Blackbird, Robin, Stonechat, Dunnock, Meadow Pipit, Rock Pipit, Starling, Greenfinch, Goldfinch, Linnet, Bullfinch, Chaffinch, House Sparrow and Goldcrest.

Plate 9 Dame Sibyl Hathaway feeding her doves in front of the now disused chapel *(M. P. Joyner)*

Plate 10 (top left) William Frederick Collings, the eccentric 21st seigneur, was thought to be responsible for the *graffiti* against vicar Seichan on the now demolished kiln *(Plate 11, top right)*. The culprit may, however, have been his younger daughter, Doris, according to the present seigneur, Michael Beaumont *(Plate 12, bottom left);* he is Collings' great-grandson.

Plate 13 (above) Churning Sark's deep yellow butter at La Tour farm early in the 1900's; some farms still make butter with more modern equipment, but the cider presses like that at Le Petit Dixcart *Plate 14 (below)* have long stopped turning.

Plate 15 La Cloche à Serk by Joshua Gosselin, August 1785. This long-forgotten landmark was to warn of impending invasion during the Napoleonic wars *(Geoffrey Gosselin)*

Plate 16 View behind Mr Le Pelley's house in Serk 1761 by Joshua Gosselin. This is now L'Ecluse *(Geoffrey Gosselin)*

Twenty definite breeding summer visitors are: the Lesser Black-backed Gull, Common Tern, Razorbill, Guillemot, Puffin, Cuckoo, Swallow, House Martin, Blackcap, Garden Warbler, Willow Warbler, Chiffchaff, Spotted Flycatcher, Lesser Whitethroat, Fulmar, Manx Shearwater, Cetti's Warbler, Dartford Warbler, Cormorant and Cirl Bunting.

The Whitethroat used to breed in fair numbers, but there is no conclusive evidence of its doing so since 1969, though a juvenile caught in 1974   seems unlikely to have been hatched outside the island.

Eleven species that formerly bred on Sark no longer do so. The Sparrowhawk and Peregrine Falcon are now seen only as vagrants; the Corncrake, Swift and Wryneck appear as passage migrants; the Kittiwake and Jackdaw as accidentals — species recorded less than ten times. The status of the Storm Petrel and Rock Dove — the latter common 300 years ago — is uncertain, while the Red-legged Partridge and Chough are now extinct in Sark.

One notable netting brought the first Channel Island sighting of the Icterine Warbler, a summer visitor to eastern and southern France. Guille ringed it in 1970 — surprisingly, three years before first netting the Melodious Warbler, a regular visitor to nearby western France.

Counts made on circuits of the island at sea and clifftop levels have established the presence of more than 2,000 pairs of Herring Gulls, a constant figure on several rechecks. Lesser Black-backed Gulls are also common, but the Great Black-backed number only 40-50 pairs. Guillemots breed on the narrow ledges of Les Autelets; their numbers vary little from year to year, though the highest count of chicks in 1974 was only twelve against eighty adults, a ratio the committee think may have been incorrect. Guillemots also have a breeding station on L'Etac. Razorbills, which visit Sark only to breed, seem to be decreasing; there were estimated to be some fifty pairs on L'Etac alone in 1946, now only ten to fifteen pairs breed here and there around the coast.

Shags are common, but the larger Cormorants — with which they are often confused by the inexperienced watcher — have been regular summer visitors to Sark only since 1976. They bred on L'Etac in 1988 and 1989. Brecqhou's Creux à Cormorans is misleading: *cormoran* in patois means Shag, a bird often shot for bait by fishermen. Apart from its bigger size, the Cormorant can be distinguished by its white chin and breeding patches.

Kittiwakes have deserted their old breeding grounds on Grosse Moie de Mouton, but the scarlet-billed Oystercatcher and Puffin are both to be found, the latter only on Moie Fano, Brenière and L'Etac. The impressive Gannet, with its wingspan of nearly 6ft, does not breed on Sark's rocks, but comes in search of food on summer visits from colonies off Alderney.

Among indigenous birds of prey is the Kestrel. In 1974 Guille nursed one back to health and flight after it was found with a broken wing. He once watched a Buzzard pluck a Starling from a loudly protesting group of companions. Only one ringed English Buzzard has ever been found outside the mainland; those visiting Sark are probably from West Germany, Scandinavia and the Baltic Countries.

A Rough-legged Buzzard, a rare passage migrant in France during the winter, spent three months in Sark during 1966, when it would float halfway across to Herm, then turn back to Grève de la Ville, soaring high like a glider.

More than one hundred 'accidental' recordings include some like the White-tailed or Sea Eagle, seen once and never likely to recur; or an occasional freak sighting during unusual weather conditions, such as a Pectoral Sandpiper in 1972. This species migrates between North and South America; occasionally some are caught by transatlantic cyclones in the gulf of Mexico and carried to the British Isles. There had been no previous sightings in the Channel Islands.

Frank Rountree's invaluable reference book *Birds of Sark* was published in 1974 and a supplement followed in 1991. This included the first sighting west of Bengal of a Siberian (Pallas's) Blue Robin by Guille in 1975, a Rose-breasted Grosbeak in the same year, Rosecoloured Starling (1978) and Little Egret (1986). The number of Sark birds is now well over two hundred.

Unhappily, both Rountree and Guille died in the late 1980s, but the work they helped revive continues. Notable new sightings in 1990 included a White Stork (May 6-25) and a Woodchat Shrike (August 22).

Rare species and scarce migrants ringed in 1980-86 had included the Nightjar, Golden Oriole, Subalpine Warbler, Dusky Warbler, Red-breasted Flycatcher, Short-toed Treecreeper, Hoopoe, Pallas's Warbler, Bonelli's Warbler, Yellow-browed Warbler, Thrush Nightingale and Scarlet Rosefinch.

A Chiffchaff ringed in Sark on October 1 1980 was recovered in Morocco two months later; a Woodcock ringed in Sark in October 1978 was recovered in Komi, USSR, five years later, and a Kestrel, ringed as a nestling in Manchester in June 1986, was recovered in Sark that September.

BUTTERFLIES AND MOTHS

Sark's communal research is now carried out by a broader-based and overdue Société Sercquiaise, formed in 1975 and parallel to the learned societies of Guernsey and Jersey. One subject worth investigation is whether the recently introduced agricultural use of pesticides has decimated the butterflies.

W. A. Luff's list of twenty-seven butterfly species on Sark in 1882 differs surprisingly little from later compilations. They were Dark Green Fritillary, Queen of Spain Fritillary,

Glanville Fritillary, Comma, Small Tortoiseshell, Large Tortoiseshell, Peacock, Red Admiral, Painted Lady, Speckled Wood, Wall, Grayling, Meadow Brown, Large Heath, Small Heath, Green Hairstreak, Small Copper, Silver Studded Blue, Brown Argus, Common Blue, Azure or Holly Blue, Pale Clouded Yellow, Clouded Yellow, Brimstone, Green Veined White, Small White and Large Garden White.

'Sark, although much smaller,' wrote Luff, 'can boast of more species than Guernsey and some of the rarer Guernsey butterflies are comparatively common there.'

In 1966, Cyril J. Shayer reported that the number of species had risen to thirty-one. Missing after eighty-four years were the Large Heath, Queen of Spain Fritillary and Pale Clouded Yellow, but there were seven additions. These were the Small Pearl-bordered Fritillary, a first Channel Island sighting in 1947 and well established by 1966; one Scarce Swallow-tail in 1934; what was claimed as the only Channel Island recording of Grizzled Skipper, mentioned in a broadcast from Sark by Brian Vesey-Fitzgerald; Swallow-tail, Orange Tip, Gatekeeper and Long-tailed Blue. The Dark Green Fritillary was still not found in Guernsey, while the Peacock appeared far more frequently on Sark than in Guernsey.

A unique 1968 sighting was the Milkweed (or Monarch), native to Central and North America, with a colossal 4in (10cm) wingspan. How it crossed the Atlantic remains a mystery, but this exotic visitor was seen on two successive days in October; the only Guernsey record of one was 102 years earlier.

A 1970 Channel Islands compilation by Roger Long listed thirty-six species as having been identified in Sark over the years. He noted that two species of Fritillary thrived there, but on no other major island; that the alleged Grizzled Skipper was almost certainly a Dingy Skipper, though this sighting remained without verification; that two Silver-washed Fritillaries had been seen on Sark in 1870 and that the only six known Channel Island records of the Mazarine Blue were in Jersey during the 1940s. Trevor Blakemore, however, claimed to have sighted the Mazarine Blue in Sark, also the Bath White, and in 1985 the Société Guernesiaise reported sighting a Lunar Hornet Clearwing, so the correct total may be thirty-nine.

A trap set in 1968 netted forty-five different species of moth, including four not previously reported in the Guernsey Bailiwick. Luff listed 125 species in 1902 and many have since been added. The larva of a Death's-head was found in 1990.

Luff's compilation, *Insects of Sark,* particularly noted the attractive Rose Chaffer beetle looking 'like living jewels as they sparkle in the sun with their heads buried in the blossom of the blackberry or the flower heads of the various plants'.

RABBITS, RATS AND SHREWS

Sark's largest wild animal is the rabbit, plentiful for centuries and a good buy for the pot at half-a-crown ($12^1\!/_2$p) some twenty years ago; but it is far rarer and generally considered inedible since myxomatosis was introduced — intentionally, according to Dame Sibyl, by one of the farmers. This foul disease is no longer so prevalent on the island, however, and the rabbit may reassert itself in a resistant strain.

There seem to be fewer rats, too. Sark's variety is the so-called Black Rat *(Rattus rattus)*, smaller, sleeker, altogether more handsome than the commoner Brown Rat that has ousted it elsewhere, though not very different in colour.

Tenant Louis Le Jeune's plea, at the 1974 Michaelmas Chief Pleas, for a bounty on rats' tails to be reintroduced indicated there may still be plenty about. The proposal was rejected, after tenant Charles Perrée commented, 'Mr Le Jeune should do the same as me, catch his own rats.' Sark does, incidentally, have a bounty *(corvid)* for rabbits, crows and magpies.

One curiosity is the Lesser White-toothed or Scilly Shrew *(Crocidura suaveolens)*, which is found also in Jersey and the Isles of Scilly, but not in Northern France, apart from islands on the Atlantic coast. The White-toothed Shrew *(Crocidura russula)*, common throughout Northern Europe, is the only species in Guernsey and Alderney, but does not appear in Jersey and Sark.

Diana Beaumont introduced hedgehogs to the Island for the first time in 1986. They quickly settled in and are thriving.

Sark has plenty of field mice, house mice and pipistrelle bats, but no moles or voles, and no reptiles. Lizards, adders, grass-snakes and slow worms, all found on the larger islands, are not indigenous to Sark, perhaps because, with its smaller land mass, it is a mainly marine habitat. There are no toads, but despite sparse surface water, frogs are numerous, both the Common and continental Nimble species.

MARINE LIFE

The sea teems with life, edible and inedible. There are fish in splendid variety: wrasse (rockfish), grey and red mullet, pollack, bass and bream to be caught with rod and line from rock platforms or over the wall at Chaussée Chenchannée. Mackerel, flatfish, dogfish, longnose, conger and whiting are plentiful offshore, with lobsters, *chancre* and spider crabs to be potted on submarine shoals like Les Moul'Chèvres. Occasionally it is even easier: fisherman Basil Adams, his boat laid up for the winter, once — on a cold December morning in a cave at Maseline — caught a marooned 20lb turbot with his bare hands.

The ormer *(Haliotis tuberculata)*, larger than the oyster, but with the same mother-of-pearl coating to its shell, is less plentiful than it used to be. These 'sea ears' *(oreilles de mer =*

ormer), found under seaweed-covered boulders uncovered by low springs, are usually prised off with a special hook. To protect the ormer against overfishing, Sark prohibits skin diving for them.

Another low-tide activity is sand-eeling; towards the end of summer, these delicately flavoured fish teem in thousands beneath the surface of the sand beaches.

The Gouliot anemones

Sark's unique feature, which attracts marine biologists to pay repeated visits, is found on the walls of the Inner Gouliot caves, glowing with vivid colours of densely packed life. Trevor Blakemore recalled a midnight picnic in 1917, when time, tide and weather combined to help him and his friends see the sea anemones 'all frosted by the light of the moon and, where the rocky pillars in the caves hid them from its light, they showed in a pale phosphorescence, a ghostly low light, reflected in the large pools through which we had to wade'.

The sea anemones are in brilliant shades of green, red, pink, yellow, orange, mauve and white, mingled with sponges and sea squirts in immense variety. Among the many species is the hydroid, *Tubularia,* with feeding polyps that open when it expands under water, as do the Dead Man's Fingers of drooping white *Alcyonium digitatum. Actinia* (Beadlet anemone), usually deep red but sometimes white, is found only here in such density, mingled with the mauve *Corynactis* and many more. One unnamed white Gouliot anemone is said to exist nowhere else; Guernsey marine biologist Roger Brehaut, still seeking it after many visits, believes this may, in fact, be *Metridium* (Plumose), usually found only offshore.

It is the vast concentration of marine life typical of deep water, on cave walls uncovered by low spring tides, that makes the Gouliots unique. Among the many other creatures are numerous crustaceans and sea spiders, but no longer any octopus to fasten on unwary legs in the pools. The octopus moved south from the Channel Islands in the late 1950s and early 1960s. The schools of porpoise that used to wheel along off the east coast have also departed. Grey seals are once-in-a-generation visitors, noted carefully in the annals of La Société Guernesiaise, like the one seen at Creux Harbour in 1909, or that caught by the two Bill Hamons, father and son, in May 1938.

THE FLORA

Sark's great variety of wild flowers are a perennial joy, but virtually nothing is known of them before the nineteenth century. The only specific mention was of a white foxglove (*Digitalis purpurea* f. *alba*), seen in 1725 by that great gardener, Thomas Knowlton. He mentions nothing else and before him there were only generalities. Helier de Carteret certainly found Sark completely overgrown in 1564, with brambles (of which there are still several species) and furze; both the Common Furze (*Ulex europaeus*) and the autumn-flowering Western species (*U. gallii*) are now present. There is evidence of the windswept tableland and valleys being treeless at that time.

The first botanical research was by Charles Babington, then in his twenties and later the revered Professor of Botany at Cambridge. In four 1838 days, 30 June to 4 July, his diary recorded 252 plants and he listed 247 in the *Primitae Florae Sarnicae* published the following year. A few were certainly not correct, among them plants typical of sandy sea coasts.

Only one other species was noted before Babington—the Sand Catchfly (*Silene conica*) by Sir W. Trevelyan in 1833. After him there was nothing more until 1892, when the inimitable Hare's-tail (*Lagurus ovatus*) was claimed. This recently reappeared in a garden, probably seeded from a dried flower arrangement.

This first list attracted other botanists to Sark, among them the Rev. W. W. Newbould, Rev. T. Salwey and E. C. Watson, forerunners of the many who will go on visiting the Channel Islands so long as the habitats of their fine and special flowers continue to be respected. But few of these able people now go to Sark, and then usually just for the short day in summer, so its flora is still not fully investigated. There seems to be suitable ground for some rarities known in the other islands, though many of the specialities have already been found.

Sark is, for example, an ideal place to see the delightful Yellow Pimpernel (*Lysimachia nemorum*), of which Jersey has only a little. The commoner plant now called Pimpernel is there in Scarlet (*Anagallis arvensis*) and at least two other colours, blue and wine-coloured, the latter a very rare form. The Bog Pimpernel (*A. tenella*), perhaps the prettiest of all with its pure pink, cup-shaped flowers, occurs in moist, heathy places. A fine patch of different coloured Pimpernels was found in a Little Sark field during 1990.

Sark's rarest wild flower is the narrow-leaved Cudweed (*Filago gallico*), not known in the other islands and very infrequently in England. People visit Sark just to see it. In one of the fields where it is found there were also, in 1957, a pretty Californian annual, Red Maids (*Calendrina ciliata*) and a Yellow Oxalis (*O. stricta*), which has been seen in only two other places in the British Isles. Neither persisted, because of later cultivation.

The only reliable Channel Island record for the rare Red Broomrape (confusingly, *Orobanche alba* in Latin, as it *can* be white) was made on Sark in 1892. It grows on Thyme (*Thymus drucei*) and badly needs refinding. Annual Knawel (*Scleranthus annuus*) is common, though rare in the other islands. Today's garden strawberries are all hybrids and one of the parents, *Fragaria chiloensis*, which comes from Chiloe off the coast of Chile, thrived on a roadside bank at Beauvoir from 1933, until it fell victim to the strimmer in recent years. Runners from the colony remain in one or two gardens.

Its first recording was by Auguste Chevalier, an eminent botanist of the Paris Natural History Museum. He also said the common Ivy on the cliffs and hedges was the Canary one, *Hedera canariensis,* not the usual English variety, *H.Helix,* a claim copied into various French works. It now seems probable that he may have confused this with the broad-leaved 'Irish' Ivy, though neither now seems to be about.

Sark shares several of the special Channel Island plants, the most obviously attractive the small, bulbous Sand Crocus (*Romulea columnae*). This grows on clifftops and opens its eyes only in the early summer sun, when its white stars would grace any garden. It cannot endure conditions in most other parts of the British Isles, so should be left in peace. Even smaller is Dwarf Rush (*Juncus capitatus*), which also flowers early and can be found by going on hands and knees in moister, short grass on cliffs and ledges, preferably with a lens to bring out its particular charm. Rare in Britain, Guernsey Chickweed (*Polycarpon tetraphyllum*) is as common as in the other islands.

Orange Bird's-foot (*Ornithopus pinnatus*), worth seeking in heathier spots, is far more delicate than the plentiful, showy Bird's Foot Trefoil (*Lotus corniculatus*). It has not been found for many years, but the search continues. One plant of Cape Cudweed (*Gnaphelium undulatum*) was found in 1912; now there are many thousands. It comes from the Cape and has been spreading in France and the islands since the early years of the last century. Not seen in England, it can be identified by the limp, pale yellow-green leaves, smelly when rubbed.

Another nineteenth century arrival was the lovely *Allium triquetrum.* Now a prevalent weed scorned as Stinking Onions, it vanishes in July. The elegant and useful sedge-like Galingale (*Cyperus longus*)—*Han* in Guernsey French—is now scarce but gave its name to the field of La Hanière, near Beauregard. It now remains only in the garden at Petit Dixcart.

Rarities and specialities apart, there is a profusion of such English favourites as massed Bluebells (*Hyacinthoides nonscripta*), Dog Violets (*Viola riviniana*) and Primroses (*Primula vulgaris*). Later come Thrift (*Armeria maritima*), Sea Campion (*Silene maritima*), Foxgloves, Ling (*Callune vulgaris*) and Bell Heather (*Erica cinerea*). Two excellent white sports of the last-named have recently been propagated.

A Check List of Sark plants, prepared by David McClintock and Frances Le Sueur, was published by La Société Guernesiaise in its *Transactions* for 1962. It listed 573 species for Sark, Brecqhou and L'Etac. A new Sark Check List is hopefully projected.

The formation of La Société Sercquiaise in 1975 gave new impetus to local interest in the flora and many new sightings include Heartsease (*Viola tricolor*), Dwarf Spurge (*Euphorbia exigus*), Blue Woodruff (*Asperula arvensis*), Ragweed (*Ambrosis artemisiifolia*) and Cockspur Grass (*Echinochloa crus-galli*). Re-found after long absence have been Deptford Pink (*Dianthus armeria*), Greater Stitchwort (*Stellaria holostea*), a single plant of Early Purple Orchid (*Orchis mascula*) and Common Eelgrass (*Zostera marina*). Among prominent new arrivals are Spring Beauty (*Montia perfolista*), Greater Celandine (*Chelidonium majus*) and Sark's own variety of Rock Sea-Lavender (*Limonium binervosum* var *serquense*).

Mosses, hepatics, lichens and seaweeds were listed by E. D. Marquand in his *Flora of Guernsey and the lesser Channel Islands* (1901) and more have since been added. Prospects of useful finds among flowering plants and ferns are good, but these so-called lower plants could provide most success. Apart, that is, from the lichens: the British Lichen Society visited Sark in 1965 and listed some 170 species. Perhaps the best field for research would be fungi. Strangely, no visiting botanist seems to have listed even one of the many species to be found.

6   THE FEUDAL SURVIVAL

'A fastness proven of old
Stands in a quaking world'
Trevor Blakemore

S ARK's remarkable degree of independence, and its tenacious attachment to laws and institutions long since abandoned elsewhere in the Western World, almost justify the subtitle, 'a Feudal State in the Twentieth Century', of Louis Selosse's invaluable 1908 study, *L'Ile de Serk*. Use of the word 'state' was perhaps a somewhat inflated description of this little island, whose anachronistic survival as a Fief Haubert—the highest kind of fief (see p 104)—has been jealously guarded by successive generations of seigneurs and tenants.

Although Sark, with Alderney, Herm and Jethou, forms part of the Guernsey Bailiwick and is ultimately subject to the lieutenant-governor of the parent island, it has its own legislature and, with periodic exceptions, manages its affairs without interference. This right was reaffirmed in the Reform (Sark) Law of 1951, under royal seal: 'Chief Pleas may make Ordinances, as heretofore, for the maintenance of public order and for the regulation of the local affairs of the island'.

CHIEF PLEAS

The Court of Chief Pleas *(Chefs Plaids)* is the island parliament, a body which votes taxes, controls finance, elects the various committees which regulate day-to-day affairs and puts forward proposals for new legislation.

Three regular meetings are held each year—on the first Wednesday after 15 January, the first Wednesday after Easter and the first Wednesday after Michaelmas. When necessary, extraordinary sessions can be convened. They take place in the senior schoolroom, members sitting on the chairs of the children enjoying an enforced holiday, the general public perched on desks at the back or standing. Behind the seigneur and his officers hangs a signed portrait of the Queen, who received Dame Sibyl's Oath of Allegiance in this room. Proceedings open and close with the Lord's Prayer, 'Notre Père, qui est aux cieux . . .', intoned in French by the greffier.

Traditionally it was a meeting of landowners, the seigneur and his tenants. The rule was one vote for each tenement— holding of land—and, as two or more came under the ownership of one person, this led to plural voting. In 1908 the seigneur owned four of the island's forty tenements and five other islanders each held two. This effectively reduced the number of voters to thirty-two, with fourteen votes in the hands of six people. The principle of one man, one vote came with the 1922 Reform Law which also established the three-yearly election by adult suffrage of twelve people's deputies. In 1991 the tenements were held by thirty-eight people. The seigneur owned two. In Little Sark, four of the five tenements are owned by the Perrée family—two by Philip snr., one by his wife, Esther, the other by his daughter, Elizabeth. Even allowing for some tenants rarely if ever attending Chief Pleas, an offence punishable by fine, this still gave landowners a decisive majority. Votes are either by show of hands or roll call, with the seigneur and then the seneschal always voting first, 'pour' or 'contre' a motion.

Legislative forms

Two forms of legislation emanate from Chief Pleas, *ordonnances* and *projets de loi*. The former (ordinances) do not require Royal Assent and can be drafted by members, then lodged with the Royal Court in Guernsey. They become law on their registration by the greffier, though the Royal Court can annul them if it considers they are unreasonable or outside the competence of Chief Pleas. Should this happen, Chief Pleas has the right of appeal to the Privy Council. The final wording is now almost invariably left to the Crown Officers in Guernsey, to ensure legal tidiness.

Projets de loi, usually concerning weightier matters, are always drawn up by the Crown Officers and require royal assent in Privy Council, after Chief Pleas has voted their acceptance or rejection.

Much Sark law still rests on ancient *lois de coutume*, customary law, based on Norman usage going back to William the Conqueror and beyond, for which the standard book of reference, kept readily to hand by the greffier, is Terrien's *Approbations des lois.* Much, however, is unwritten.

Seigneur's role in Chief Pleas

Apart from voting first, being able to delay an ordinance by veto for twenty-one days and his appointment of officers, the seigneur has the same rights and duties in Chief Pleas as other members. When Dame Sibyl died, there was conjecture in the British Press as to whether her grandson and successor, Michael Beaumont, would bring major changes—for instance, by allowing motor cars on the island. This was based on the mistaken belief that the seigneur held absolute power. In fact, he can only *propose* changes to the law, like any other voting members of Chief Pleas. The *decision* is by vote of the corporate body, even if some members may follow the lead given by him.

He does, however, appoint the four chief officers of the island: seneschal, greffier, treasurer and prévôt, with the approval of the lieutenant-governor, but without reference to Chief Pleas.

Seneschal

The seneschal's term of office is three years, during which he cannot be removed, except at his own request or by direction of the Crown, and he can be reappointed for further terms. He is sworn in by the lieutenant-governor.

Apart from his position as president of Chief Pleas — at which he is the only person to vote by other than landowning or elected right and where he holds an additional casting vote — the seneschal's role is one of special importance. He summons Chief Pleas to its regular meetings and can call extraordinary ones with the seigneur's consent.

His greatest authority, however, is as the sole judicial executive or magistrate. His court, which deals with both civil and petty criminal cases, has been effective since 1675, when a patent of Charles II abolished the court of five jurats elected by the people of Sark. In criminal cases the seneschal can sentence wrongdoers to three days and two nights in the Sark jail. He can impose fines up to £1,000 and imprisonment up to two months, to be served in Guernsey.

When there was a serious outbreak of arson and brigandage in 1891-2, the seneschal assumed the role of senior police officer and instituted an official inquiry, aided by a Guernsey police detective and two lawyers. He also fulfils the functions of coroner. The seneschal's authority is all-embracing; not even the seigneur who appointed him can escape his judgement, if the case arises. His salary in 1991 was increased to £5,895; in 1960 it had been only £600. He swears in the greffier, treasurer and prévôt, who, unlike him, are appointed *sine die*. All four offices are part-time. The present seneschal is an electrical engineer, the greffier the Island blacksmith, the treasurer landlord of the Bel Air and the prévôt a fisherman.

Greffier and treasurer

The offices of greffier and treasurer can be held by the same person, as they were from 1951 to 1978. In 1991 each carried a salary of £3,370. They have seats in Chief Pleas, but cannot vote. The greffier keeps the official records, both of Chief Pleas and the seneschal's court, and has his own office building, the Greffe. His functions combine those of town clerk and clerk of the court.

Prévôt

The prévôt, too, has a non-voting seat in Chief Pleas, but his role there is obscure. His duties are to carry out decisions of the seneschal's court by collecting fines and supervising jail sentences. He is responsible for feeding prisoners and, when offenders are committed to Guernsey, for delivering them to the authorities in St Peter Port. His 1991 salary was £1,584; £719 more than in 1960. The prévôt was traditionally entitled, according to Selosse, to keep part or all of the fines imposed by the seneschal, but this no longer applies.

Constables

Two constables, the *connétable* and the *vingtenier*, are elected by each Michaelmas Chief Pleas to maintain law and order, among many other duties. The *vingtenier* is the junior constable, replacing the *connétable*, who then stands down, at the end of his first year in office. Their functions are identical, except that the vingtenier cannot spend public money. Both are honorary posts, but in recent years they have been compensated for lost working time by a fixed annual expenses allowance—£1,244 for the connétable and £369 for the vingtenier in 1991.

They have the right of arrest and the duty to conduct prisoners before the seneschal, or, if the offence is at a late hour—as, with cases of drunkenness, is not unlikely—to keep them in jail overnight. Their role ends when the court passes sentence and the prévôt's duties begin.

Selosse says the constables were obliged to act on complaints laid before them; if they refused to do so, the seneschal could instruct the prévôt provisionally to replace them. This seems no longer to be the case. The constables have no uniform, but since 1803 have been issued with maces as badges of office.

SEIGNEURIAL RIGHTS

The privileges of the seigneur, as lord of the manor, remain much as they were when the fief was granted by Queen Elizabeth I. The fief itself is indivisible and hereditary by primogeniture, though it may be sold by express permission of the Crown. Unlike the United Kingdom, the title goes with the land, not the land with the title. Like all feudal institutions, the granting of the fief of Sark had military origins—to protect the Queen's possession of the island by British subjects numerous and disciplined enough for the purpose. The seigneur was entitled to grant, within his fief, *bails à rente*, properties given in perpetuity for an annual rental—the origin of Sark's forty tenements.

The Seigneur's own annual Michaelmas payment to the Crown, one-twentieth of a Knight's Service Fee, is equivalent to £1.79. On inheriting the fief, or buying it, he makes an additional token payment of *première saisine*. The seigneur draws no salary from the island and his main source of income is a levy on sales of property, one-thirteenth part of the purchase price, *le treizième*. Its record during the past century reflects rocketing property values.

Between 1860 and 1919, no land was sold by the seigneurs, but other sales totalled more than £47,000 and the *treizième* averaged about £65 for each of the sixty years. From 1919 to 1966 seigneurial sales—including those of Brecqhou, Le Manoir and L'Ecluse—were £19,390; other sales were over £442,000 and the average yearly income from the *treizième* had risen to about £700. But from 1967 to 1974 sales of property not belonging to Dame Sibyl fetched well in excess of £400,000 and the *treizième* became worth almost £4,000 a year, while in 1989/90 Michael Beaumont collected £33,461.54. The amount for 1980 had been £34,069.23.

When a tenement is sold, the *congé*, or approval of the seigneur, must be obtained and his permission given in writing on the *contrat* of sale, many of which are in French. Dame Sibyl refused her *congé* three times in forty-seven years; Beaumont has yet to do so.

Michael Beaumont inherited from her various other rights and tithes, apart from those *rentes* which had not then been redeemed by a once-for-all payment. None is worth very much in hard financial terms. There was a time, for instance, when the seigneur employed a woman called *la dîmeresse* to attend harvesting at all farms and ensure that his *dîme*, every tenth sheaf of corn, came to him. It would certainly not pay him to do so nowadays. The tithe of *poulage*, a live chicken annually to the seigneur is still in force, though payment is usually now in money ('I fix the exchange rate very low, as I don't really want a scraggy chicken,' Michael Beaumont). *Rente* is also given in terms of wheat, barley, oats and, in two cases only, money. The income totals a modest £250 yearly. The *droit du tavernage*, entitling the seigneur to grant liquor licences, no longer exists. The monopoly of milling rights and the tithe on lambs and wool were also enforced by Dame Sibyl, but other feudal dues and privileges were allowed to lapse.

But the seigneur can call upon anyone at any time to take the oath of allegiance and he can deport any persons after forty days, if they have not his permission to remain on the island. Only he can keep bitches, pigeons or doves. His rights extend three miles seaward from Sark's foreshore; Dame Sibyl once stopped a Guernsey boat running excursions to the Gouliot caves, because its passengers were not paying the landing toll. He retains the right to nominate Sark's vicar, but cannot dismiss him.

PROPERTY RIGHTS AND INHERITANCE

After signature of the *contrat,* when a tenement is sold, the transfer is passed, field by field, in the seneschal's court, then signed by the seneschal and registered by the greffier. Any kinsman up to a seventh degree of affinity—some references say five degrees, but Terrien stipulates seven— can reclaim the property by exercising the right of *retraite lignager* and paying, within a specified period, a price equivalent to that of the purchase.

There have been countless disputes about property rights. One, about ownership of a field in 1898, led to Jean Hamon raising *Le Clameur de Haro* for what appears to have been the last time in Sark. The *clameur,* common to all the Channel Islands may possibly have originated with Duke Rollo of Normandy (Ha, Rollo, hence 'Haro'). If the injured party in the presence of witnesses cries 'Haro, Haro, Haro! A l'aide mon Prince, on me fait tort,' the alleged offence is automatically halted until it can be brought to court. A dispute concerning the inheritance rights of Le Port à la Jument tenement (Vaudin *v* Hamon and Mesny) had been, by 1982, the subject of litigation for fourteen years without being resolved. It never was fully.

Laws defining land tenure are precise, but they have not always been strictly observed. Tenants may not divide their land, or bequeath any part of it. Unless sold during the tenant's lifetime, the tenement passes to the heir by primogeniture, free of mortgage, encumbrance or debt, with the exception of the annual seigneurial dues and rentes. If no heir can be found within the seventh degree of affinity, the tenement reverts to the seigneur.

A male tenant's widow is protected by right of *douaire*, which entitles her to one-third of her husband's land, house furniture and money during her lifetime and she pays one-third of the *rente* and seigneurial dues. The husband of a woman tenant has an even better umbrella, *franc veuvage*, under which he can occupy the whole of his late wife's property during his lifetime, or until he remarries, providing there are living issue.

WOMEN'S RIGHTS

As divorce was not recognised, by Sark law until 1977, the children of any second marriage contracted outside the island were deemed illegitimate and without rights. This caused hardship, as did laws which, until recently, governed the position of married women. Husband and wife were regarded as one person, the wife's legal entity as part of her husband's, her personal chattels vested in him. She could not legally have a joint bank account or hold stocks and shares jointly with her husband—though these provisions were often flouted—nor could she dispose of moveable property (ie other than real estate) without her husband's consent. She had no right to hold a separate personal estate, nor could she dispose of such estate by will or otherwise.

Even in feudal Sark this situation eventually provoked strong feminist reaction. Considering how long it usually takes to make major changes, the Women's Rights

Committee, under its bank manager chairman, Deputy John York, had remarkable success in getting a centuries-old situation reversed in little more than twelve months—and by the surprising majority of two-to-one in the male-dominated Chief Pleas. Three new projets de loi, approved at an extraordinary meeting in November 1974, ended the discrimination against women.

A married woman with children can now dispose of personal moveable property in the following way: one-third to the surviving spouse, one-third to the children and one third freely by will. The portion divided equally between the children is *le légitime*. Where there are no children, half the property goes to the surviving spouse and half is freely disposable. In the case of a husband or wife already widowed, the children are entitled to half the property and half can be bequeathed by will. The new law was based on similar legislation which had worked well in Guernsey for fifty years, without dispute or further amendments. What the Sark law omitted from the Guernsey version, however, was all reference to a married women being allowed to dispose by will of real estate, or *immovable* property, in the island. That would have cut across the ancient laws of inheritance, which are the unique bedrock of Sark land tenure and the Women's Rights Committee emphasised this was never its intention.

A married woman was, additionally, legally enabled to run a business under her own name and to enjoy its profits; she could enjoy her own savings and her profits from any employment or occupation. Her husband, in return, was freed from his previous responsibility for her debts.

ADOPTION AND DIVORCE

Children adopted under Guernsey law, or law recognised in Guernsey, were, under the women's rights legislation, given the same rights as natural children of their adoptive parents, but forfeited any claim to inherit from their natural parents. This applies only to outsiders settling in Sark with adopted children, as the island has no adoption laws of its own.

Divorce was long unrecognised because of its apparent threat to inheritance rights and these were given specific protection when it finally came into force. Dame Sibyl, towards the end of her life, considered it would be preferable to let Sark come under Guernsey law in this particular, as lack of divorce facilities made life difficult for some of the island. More than twenty couples lived together without a marriage licence, a situation involving little moral stricture in Sark's tolerant climate, but one that did cause legal hardship. In 1976 a working party began to investigate the question of divorce and in January 1977 Chief Pleas agreed to recognise divorces granted outside the Island. The granting of divorce on Sark was rejected, but generally the islanders are happy in their 'state' of suspended historical animation.

7   EARLY HISTORY

'. . . they are worse than Cannibals'
Rabelais

ACCOUNTS of Sark history before the mid-sixteenth century are fragmentary and often contradictory. Folklore is interwoven with detail from legal and ecclesiastical records and for long periods the only inhabitants appear to have been pirates.

PREHISTORIC SARK

Two surviving dolmens provide evidence of burials taking place in prehistoric times. They were identified in 1974 by David E. Johnston, tutor in archaeology at Southampton University's Department of Extra Mural Studies. The larger (Grid ref: WV 45767350), near the clifftop above Brenière bay, is clearly visible from the sea and has long been known to local fishermen as an ancient monument. A massive capstone, roughly triangular in section and measuring 12ft 4in x 11ft 6in (3.75 x 3.50m), is supported by five of the ten crude boulders below to form a roughly constructed cist. The nineteenth-century Guernsey archaeologist, F. C. Lukis, knew the site, regarded it as artificial, but left no written record; Kendrick's *The Archaeology of the Channel Islands* does not mention it.

Another roughly-built cist (Grid ref: WV 45457429) has a much smaller capstone supported on three squat uprights and some smaller boulders, with an exposed outcrop of rock forming the rear of the structure. It stands on a cliffside plateau above the southern end of Vermandaie bay. Kendrick, who never visited the site, apparently believed the formation to be natural, but again local opinion held it to be man-made, a view shared by Johnston. His guide to Channel Island archaeological sites gives fuller descriptions and diagrams of these monuments.

The dolmens were probably those noted by Cachemaille a century ago: '. . . not many years since, the whereabouts of ten cromlechs could be perfectly distinguished, but all have now disappeared with the exception of two nearly entire cysts. A few great stones, which originally belonged to these cromlechs may still be seen here and there, the rest have been broken up to construct walls and houses.' Some huge gateposts, such as those at La Hèche, the Collenette entrance to The Avenue—once the gated approach to Le Manoir—may, like the large stones at Vaurocque crossroads, be relics of the dismantled monuments.

Cachemaille also mentioned the unearthing of many different sized stone troughs and mullers, as well as 'quantities of stone knives, hammers, hatchets, amulets or discs of stone and clay beads'. Kendrick believed Sark may 'have been occupied continuously throughout the Megalithic period (2000-1000 BC) and up to Roman times . . . the place was inhabited at the beginning of the Metal Era, for a flat copper axe was found on Little Sark, the principal source of the raw metal and . . . the tip of a bronze axe, perhaps a fragment from a founder's stock, also comes from this island'. Cachemaille reported ancient Celtic pottery discovered in the last century, embedded in cinders 2-3ft below ground level.

UNDER THE ROMANS

An earthenware pot, dug up by chance near the mill in 1719, contained thirteen round and oblong pieces of metal, some with a fish motif, and eighteen small coins, probably from the first century BC. Known as the 'Sark Hoard', the find was sent to absentee seigneur Lord John Carteret in Bedfordshire. Engravings of the coins later identified them as of Gaulish origin, possibly brought to Sark by refugees from Caesar's wars of conquest, or even by his Roman legionaries.

During the Roman Empire the islands came under an administrative centre at Constantia, now the Norman town of Coutances. Sark's Roman name has appeared variously as Sarmia, Sarnia and Sargia, with Besargia attributed either to Little Sark or Brecqhou. Some writers believe Sarnia was Guernsey, and Sark references in medieval documents are often to *Insula Sargiensis*.

ST MAGLOIRE'S MONASTERY

In the fourth century AD, when the Romans officially adopted Christianity, the islands became part of the Coutances bishopric, a link that persisted until 1567. Sark's first contact with Christian evangelism, however, probably dates from the arrival of St Magloire, reputedly in AD565, exactly 1,000 years before Elizabeth I granted the island's royal charter.

The missionary saint is said to have been born in the bishopric of Vannes, the son of Afrella, a Welsh princess, and Umbrafel, himself the son of Emyr Lhydau, a Breton seigneur. One story claims Sark was uninhabited when Magloire ('son of glory') arrived to found his monastery; a second says the saint was given half the island in exchange for his miraculous cure of Count Loyesco, while Magloire was Bishop of Dol in Brittany; according to a third version, Sark was governed at the time by a petty sovereign *(regulus)*, Badwall (or Radwal), who granted Magloire land there. Loyesco is probably synonymous with Comte l'Oiseau, Lord of Jersey, who—in yet another account—encouraged Magloire to make his missionary voyage.

While on Sark, the saint is reputed to have cured of dumbness the daughter of a Guernseyman named Nivo and, in a nice blend of spiritual succour and materialism, to have exacted one-third of Nivo's property in payment. A 1928 pamphlet, *Notes on Feudal Tenure* by Dame Sibyl, lists 'the Lords of Sark so far as at present known', including 'AD550—Nivo (a nobleman who chose Sark as his burial place and who seems to have held possession of West Sark)' and 'AD580—Count l'Oiseau (probably a descendant of Nivo)'.

Sark's monastery, established during the latter half of the sixth century, became a seat of learning for children of noblemen on the near-by French coast. One charming story, from a tenth-century document, tells how some of these children were playing in the hulk of an abandoned boat, when a tidal wave carried them out to sea. Their prayers were answered when Magloire appeared, walking on the water, and guided the boat to a foreign kingdom with his crook. Some days later the derelict boat, laden with the king's rich gifts of grain, flour, wool and clothing, returned to Sark. 'St Magloire,' commented Cachemaille, 'was not insensible to the generous present.'

The monks built a watermill in the valley below their monastery in north-west Sark, damming a stream to make three reservoirs, which were stocked with carp and provided power for the mill to grind corn grown in fields near the present Seigneurie. One pond survives and a few names recall the monks' labours: La Moinerie (monastery), L'Ecluse (dam), Port du Moulin (mill port). 'Port' suggests a harbour, but L'Eperquerie is generally thought to have been the only landing place.

Magloire died between AD585 and 617, according to varying records, which also give differing versions of his departure. One says his body was moved to Jersey, another

(*Acta Sanctorum Octubris*) that it lay peacefully in Sark until around AD850, when six Breton monks opened the grave and took the corpse to Léhon, near Dinan in Brittany. The local king, Nominöe, had promised them land to build a priory on condition they brought a saint's remains as security. Their successful mission led to the foundation of the famous Royal Priory of Léhon, where Magloire's remains rested until eventually removed to Paris.

St Guénault is believed to have taken Christianity from Sark to Alderney and was long that island's patron saint.

The Sark monastery attracted little outside attention until marauding Norsemen reached the Channel Islands about the middle of the ninth century and sacked church buildings. It may have been a band under the command of Danish chieftain Jarl Hastings who destroyed the monastery, killing the monks and their young pupils. The events were recalled in a medieval poem:

> Sargi et le lieux furent envais
> de paiens et mau le menèrent
> et cruellement le devastèrent
> Au moustier saint Magloire vinrent
> à grand crix et grant braierie . . .

(. . . All of Sark was overrun by heathens, who caused much woe and cruelly devastated it; to the monastery of St Magloire they came, with a great cry and great tumult.)

It recounts how seven infidels, trying to break open Magloire's tomb, were blinded, while another 900 lost heart for the battle and slew each other—probably a variation of the Breton monks' legend.

A pile of stones in the Seigneurie grounds, according to superstition, came from Magloire's original cell in Sark— and woe betide anyone who moves it! Magloire appears in a modern, stained-glass window in St Peter's Church, dedicated to members of the Hotton family, while his name survives in that of a twentieth-century house off Rue Lucas.

MEDIEVAL ADMINISTRATION

Jersey-born poet Robert Wace, who died in 1184, wrote *Le Roman de Rou* in Norman French, recalling the ravages of the Norsemen: ' . . . En Aurenen, en Guernesi,/En Saire, en Erm, en Gersi . . .' (in Alderney, Guernsey, Sark, Herm and Jersey). The barbarians eventually embraced local customs, including the Frankish *fiefs* of land and privileges granted by a sovereign in exchange for pledged loyalty, an annual rental and armed support.

Le Comte de Gerville's *Iles du Cotentin* says: "There formerly existed, and probably may still exist in the archives of Mont St Michel, provisionally deposited in the library of the town of Avranches, a charter of Néel, whereby he gave to this abbey his woods, situated in the island of Sark'. The charter was dated 942, a year given for Néel being 'Lord of Sark' in Dame Sibyl's pamphlet. She presumably used the de Gerville reference, but the charter's Latin text may have referred to Guernsey, not Sark, and there were no woods on Sark 600 years later.

William Long-Sword, son of Norse chieftain Duke Rollo of Normandy, was granted the Channel Islands by the French Crown in AD933. A later Duke of Normandy, Robert, granted the fief of Guernsey to the Abbey of Mont St Michel in 1030; but in 1042 the guardian of Robert's under-age son, William the Bastard (later William the Conqueror) revoked the gift and substituted the isles of Alderney and Sark. In 1057 William, by then of age, transferred Alderney and Sark to Geoffrey de Moubrai, Bishop of Coutances. Sark must have supported a settled community, as the title to its tithes had been sold to the Bishop of Avranches about 1045.

Church rights on Sark, confused by the island changing hands with the fortunes of warring kings and nobles, were the subject of litigation over many years. The abbey of Mont St Michel still claimed its title to Alderney and Sark as late as 1178 and Assize Rolls for 1238 ('Pleas at Sark of the same Eyre on Thursday next after the Octaves of St John . . .') record the case of 'Nicholas, Bishop of Avranches, concerning a plea of the advowson of (two holdings?) of the Church of Sark'.

The Norman Conquest of 1066 brought the Channel Islands into an association with the English Crown that, with only brief interruptions, has persisted to the present day.

The de Vernon fief

The warring Bishop de Moubrai forfeited Sark in 1093, after supporting an unsuccessful revolt of English barons against William Rufus. It returned to the Duchy of Normandy and, in the reign of Henry I, appears to have passed to the king's loyal supporter, Richard de Reviers, together with the title of 'Guardian to the Abbey of Montebourg in the Cotentin'. A surviving charter shows that Sark later belonged to Richard's second son, William de Vernon, whose main estate was at Vernon-sur-Seine. Other contemporary charters speak of the presence in Sark of *hospîtes,* immigrants given land to develop round the site of the old monastery, and of a priest appointed to the Parish Church of St Mary—perhaps the chapel in the Seigneurie grounds, where David Johnston recently discovered shreds of Norman pottery. He made similar finds near the old windmill in Little Sark. The priest's living came from the Bishop of Coutances.

No move to restore the monastery was made under the de Vernons, and William's propitiatory gifts of revenue from agriculture and the watermill went to the Abbey of Montebourg. In exchange, Montebourg sent a monk to say mass for the souls of the de Vernons, William supplying him with pasturage and straw to heat his cell. The use of straw suggests that gorse or furze, later Sark's main fuel, may not then have been growing there.

The lone monk's priory was a one-cell building and, like the monastery, bore St Magloire's name. A charter under the seal of William's son, Richard de Vernon, confirmed the monk's position in 1196, raising his income.

A growing community

Basing his estimate on de Vernon revenues, Selosse put Sark's population at the beginning of the thirteenth century at more than 400. To support that number, much of the island must have been under cultivation.

In 1203 the English Crown stripped Richard of the fief when he switched his allegiance to King Philippe Auguste of France, who had conquered the Duchy of Normandy, apart from the Channel Islands.

Another turncoat, pirate mercenary Eustache (or Wistache) le Moine, briefly restored Sark to France. Commissioned by King John of England to reconquer Normandy, Eustache and his cut-throat crews of English, Flemish and even French sailors ravaged the coasts of north-west France from 1204 to 1211. He then quarrelled with John and was given command of a large fleet by the French king, with the aim of restoring the Channel Islands to the Duchy. They occupied Sark in 1212 and 1216, but were finally evicted in 1218 by the English Crown's Warden of the Islands, Philippe d'Aubigny (d'Albini). The 7ft thick walls at La Seigneurie may have formed part of the fortifications built against renewed French attacks.

Forfeiture of the de Vernon estates was confirmed by Henry III in 1230 and four years later the king gave his 'beloved Richard, Vicar of St Mary in Sark' the church tithes in perpetuity. For the next hundred years Sark appears to have supported a well-established and reasonably prosperous community. Assize Rolls mention two erring publicans '. . . le Roseye, taverners of wine and ale . . . and

Peter le Parmenter junior, taverner and baker, have transgressed . . . ' Among tenants owing *rentes* to the Crown, were Henry Warren, Ralph Odo, Richard du Port, Richard Néel, Ralph de la Croix, Colin du Val, Geoffrey le Moigne and Ralph Mynot. Fishing was thriving and there are references to several *éperqueries,* where the fish were hung to dry before being salted down for export.

Administration was in the hands of a prévôt, appointed by the Warden of the Islands. His first duty was to collect revenue due to the king from *rentes* and dues, including the *champart* levied at Michaelmas on every twelfth sheaf of corn and bundle of flax, and *panage* for every pig over one year old. Richard Durel; Ralph, son of Odo , and William, son of Richard, were three of the prévôts in the last decade of the thirteenth century and the beginning of the fourteenth. Another part of their duties was to preside over the king's court, composed of a bedel and six jurats chosen for life. The prévôt's position was, in many ways, similar to those of the present-day seneschal, greffier and treasurer combined, rather than to the official now holding the same title.

FRENCH OCCUPATIONS

A sudden decline in Sark's fortunes came when France's Scottish allies under David Bruce invaded the island in 1337, setting fire to buildings and crops, and murdering many of the inhabitants. In the following year Guernsey, Alderney and Sark were captured by French admiral Nicolas Bahuchet and occupied until 1340. Another occupation, by naval forces under Luis de la Cerda lasted from 1343 to 1347, and the Black Death then brought even worse miseries.

Sark's defence against de la Cerda seems to have rested hopefully on one armed man and half-a-dozen archers kept there by Thomas of Hampton (Warden,1341-3)! A report to

Plate 17 Looking across Baleine Bay to La Pointe Derrible from Le Pôt

Plate 18 Gouliot headland and La Moie au Sieur Peter, with the path to the Gouliot caves in the foreground

Plate 19 Inner Gouliot cave, its walls encrusted with anemones (*John Morton, 1902*)

Plate 20 An Edwardian outing to the main Boutique cave (*John Morton, 1903*)

Plate 21 Landing from the *Alert* in Creux Harbour during the early 1900s *(John Morton)* and *Plate 22* Waiting to embark at Maseline some eighty years later *(The British Tourist Authority)*

Plate 23 The photographer's wife and noveliest John Oxenham by the dolmen above Brenière bay and *Plate 24* Vraic being unloaded at Creux Harbour for use as manure *(John Morton, 1907)*. Morton's pictures illustrated the first edition of *Carette of Sark* by Oxenham

the English Crown by John de Roches some years earlier had claimed that nature rendered Sark impregnable.

The popular version of Sark's 'Trojan Horse' story probably dates from this grim period. It relates how would-be invaders obtained permission to land and bury a passenger who had died at sea. The coffin contained not a corpse, but weapons; the raiders opened it in the Chapel, armed themselves and slew the Sarkese wholesale. One version of the story, from an old Latin manuscript, quoted in Falle's *History of Jersey*, says the ruse was used by English seamen from Rye and Winchelsea in Sussex, avenging Sarkese wrecking of ships by the use of false lights. Sir Walter Raleigh's *History of the World* places the incident, almost certainly wrongly, during Sark's recapture from the French in the sixteenth century.

The Treaty of Brétigny (1360), under which Edward III handed over his Norman rights to the French, brought Sark a brief respite. French attacks on the Channel Islands— which England retained— were soon resumed, however, and to devastating effect. William de Asthorpe, rendering account of Channel Islands revenue to February 1374, included the item of 112 sols tournois for Sark, adding that no more could be expected 'because the said Island is so destroyed by the wars that there is no revenue to be derived from it save for the hunting of rabbits'.

Pirates' haven

Mutilated accounts of Thomas of Appleby, Receiver of the Channel Islands 1374-7, show that Sark was then being farmed, and Cachemaille believed revenues received by Henry VI proved it was inhabited and under cultivation as late as 1461. There is little evidence, however, of Sark being used other than for rabbiting expeditions from Guernsey, pasturage and as a haven for pirates until 1549.

Rabelais, who sailed near Sark during the 1530s, wrote in *Pantagruel:* 'Let us never descend to the lands of thieves and robbers . . . I assure you that is the case here . . . in the islands of Sark and Herm, between Brittany and England . . . isles of pirates, thieves, brigands, murderers and assassins . . . let us not go there, I beg you . . . they kill boys for beef, worse than cannibals. They would eat us all alive.'

Fortifications

The English government carried out extensive defensive works in Jersey, Guernsey and Alderney during the 1540s and paid the price for missing out Sark. Some 200 paroled convicts, under the command of Captain François Breuil (or Bruel) were landed there in 1549 by a French naval force, which then raided Jersey. Reinforced by another 200 men under Breuil's brother a month later, the Frenchmen built three small forts in Sark, on sites probably originally used by the Norsemen: Le Grand Fort in the north; Château des Quénevêts on the Hog's Back, and Vermandaie on the west coast of Little Sark.

The Frenchmen, whose numbers had by then fallen to less than 100, were driven out in 1553 by Adrian Crole, a Flemish corsair, acting in connivance with Guernsey's Lieutenant-Governor, Thomas Compton. The anonymous *Chronicles of Jersey* relates that Queen Mary gave Crole and his companions no reward for their enterprise, but a landing party was sent from Jersey to demolish the forts— 'they returned to Jersey', it adds, 'leaving the Isle of Sark once more vacant, no one in those insecure days being found desirous of risking life or property on so isolated a spot'.

The permanent settlement of Sark was only ten years away, however; it followed a final, and short-lived French occupation. In 1560 the seigneur of Glatigny, in Normandy, was given permission by the French king to establish a colony in Sark; but the Normans departed once more after a fresh outbreak of Anglo-French hostilities in 1562.

8 FORTY MEN WITH MUSKETS

'. . . for term or terms of life,
lives, years, for ever or otherwise.'
Queen Elizabeth's Letters Patent

HELIER DE CARTERET

SARK's outline was clearly visible from St Ouen in Jersey, the fief of Helier de Carteret, a nephew and son-in-law of the former bailiff, who had been prominent in encouraging the Protestant religion and was well regarded at the English court.

Realising the dangers to Jersey of the French reoccupying Sark, or of it again becoming a refuge for pirates, Helier wondered if he could both prevent this and gain future profit for himself by colonising the island. In September 1563, he was granted permission to do so by the Crown Commissioners and Captain of Guernsey, on payment of 50 sols tournois. The sol (or sou) was one-twentieth part of the livre tournois; twelve deniers made up one sol, and eight doubles one denier—measurements similar to pounds, shillings and pence. The livre tournois fluctuated from parity with the pound sterling in 1470 to about 1s 8d, or 8p, in recent times. Even at its highest valuation, Helier's was a mere peppercorn payment.

Trial cultivation of a small parcel of land in 1564 convinced him that Sark's soil would be richly productive, and in the following year he and his wife, Margaret, went to settle there. The formidable difficulties facing them were detailed, probably by a later de Carteret, in the *Chronicles of Jersey:*

... they had to carry with them all that was needed, such as bread, drink, wheat, grain, salt, beer, wine, cider, food and all other substance; the whole of which they had to convey by water. There was in all the Island neither house nor home; excepting a little vaulted chapel where the Seigneur with his Lady and followers took shelter till they had found means to reconstruct some stone walls near the chapel, where a church had formerly stood, more than two hundred years before. Here they erected a dwelling place which they thatched with fern to keep out the rain and wind, whilst they sent for wood, reed, straw and all other requisites for building houses, not only for themselves but for their people.

They likewise sent for horses and oxen to plough the ground; and for cows to increase their stock of provisions by the addition of milk and butter; and for wood to build their houses, and to make ploughs and carts, spades, forks, and all the other necessary implements for the tillage and cultivation of the land; as also wood to burn and trees to plant. Everything had to traverse the sea which caused enormous outlay. Besides all this, the Island was covered with rabbit warrens, fernbrakes, heaths, brambles, thorns, and every sort of brushwood, so that it was a mere waste, and the prospect of bringing it into cultivation seemed hopeless. There was not even a road nor any kind of way by which a cart might pass; neither was there any harbour where the boats might be unloaded without immense expenditure of time, pains and money.

The chapel of the *Chronicles* was a former priory. On its site the de Carterets built Le Manoir, in the centre of Great Sark, looking out towards their home in St Ouen.

ROYAL LETTERS PATENT

The de Carterets' first year in Sark happily coincided with peace between England and France. Helier obtained from Queen Elizabeth the Letters Patent, delivered under the Great Seal of England at Greenwich on 6 August 1565, that determined the future form of Sark society.

The Letters recalled the Crown's loss of 'the ancient and accustomed profits, rents, revenues, incomes and emoluments from thence long since' and that Sark had become a haven for England's enemies in wartime and for pirates in times of peace. To ensure the island's future safety and wellbeing as a place '. . . occupied, possessed and inhabited by Englishmen and others of Our natural subjects' it was granted 'with all its rights and privileges' to Helier and his heirs for an annual payment of 'the twentieth part of a Knight's Fee . . on the Feast of the Archangel St Michael' and in consideration of the 50 sols tournois already paid.

The rights and privileges were all-embracing. They included:

> . . . all manner of tithes, oblations, fruits, obventions, mines, quarries, ports, shores, rocks, wrecks of the sea, shipwrecks, farms, fee-farms, knights' fees, wards, marriages, escheates, reliefs, heriots, goods and chattels waived, goods and chattels of felons, fugitives or pirates, or felons de se, outlaws, of persons put in exigent, and the forfeited or confiscated goods of persons condemned or convicted anyway whatsoever; also all forfeitures, paunages, free warrens, courts leet, views of frank pledge, assize and assay of bread, wine and beer; all fairs, markets, customs, rights of tolls, jurisdictions, liberties, immunities, exemptions, franchises, privileges, commodities, profits, emoluments, and all the Queen's heredits whatsoever with every of their appurts . . .

There were only two conditions. Firstly, that Sark should within two years be occupied by at least forty men; secondly, that the island should not be sold or pass out of Helier de Carteret's family without Crown consent.

TENANTS AND LEASES

Helier had to act quickly to fulfil the two-year provision. Apart from his early proof of Sark's agricultural potential, its overgrown wasteland was not an alluring prospect for the kind of steady, young family man he needed. The terms of the royal charter, however, provided the answer by entitling him 'to lease, grant and farm some parts or parcels of the said island of Serk by indentures to be sealed with his seal or theirs, for term or terms of life, lives, years, for ever or otherwise.'

Helier realised that the right type of settler would be attracted by the opportunity to acquire what amounted to freehold property on potentially rich farmland. He divided Sark into parcels, called *tènements,* each with its own coastal strip of *côtils,* or cliff grazing, and each with the obligation for its tenant to build a house and supply a man armed with a musket and ammunition for the island's defence. The shrewd Jerseyman took for his own family the key, central position of some 300 vergées (140 acres).

The second biggest holding, on the west coast, went to Nicolas Gosselin, a Guernsey jurat who had been his ally in negotiations with the Crown Commissioners and whose father, Helier Gosselin, had moved from Jersey to become a notoriously cruel bailiff of Guernsey.

The Gosselin tenement of Beauregard itself formed a sub-fief and Nicolas divided it in four, retaining the largest part (now Grand Beauregard) and taking as tenants three men who came with him from Guernsey: Noel Vaudin, Guillaume Tanquerel and Nicholas du Val.

Gosselin's lease, far more favourable than others drawn up by de Carteret, granted freedom from corn tithes and the right to one-half of all *gravage* (materials washed up by the sea) on the coast bounding his estate. He was also allowed to hunt over his land—the lone exception to the seigneur's monopoly of *le droit à la chasse* elsewhere in the island. In return he had to provide four men with muskets while he and his heirs continued to live on the island, or at least five if they went to reside elsewhere. His name survives at Havre Gosselin, where he moored his boat.

Jersey colonists

Apart from the Beauregard settlement and his own holding, Helier created thirty-five tenements, five of them in Little Sark. Some were only 10 vergées, others four times that size, but all included the coastal strip which their tenants were pledged to defend. The Seigneur de Glatigny had been threatening to reassert his own right to Sark, so Helier kept his men on the alert.

They enclosed their fields by planting hedges, like those in Jersey, from which most of the men came. When they arrived there were no hedges on Sark, an indication that medieval agriculture had been of the open-field pattern.

Each lease, granted in perpetuity, carried an annual rental of one cabot of wheat for each vergée of cultivable land. Tithes included two capons annually; every tenth sheaf of corn, barley and oats; a tenth part of bean, pea, vetch, flax, hemp and apple crops; and a levy on lambs and wool.

Some colonists from Jersey—like Guillaume Chevalier, Jean Le Cerf, Jean Vibert, François Le Couteur, Pierre Rogier, Jean Guille, Jean Le Brocq and Nicolas Cristin—were natives of Helier's own fief, St Ouen. Two—Hiou and Julien de Carteret—were relatives of his. From other parts of Jersey came Thomas Poindestre, Pierre Le Feuvre, Jacques Dolbel, Thomas Hamon and Jehannet Hotton . The present seigneurie, then known as La Perronerie and named after the *perron* or wide flight of steps in front of the house, was the holding of Isaac Le Gros.

Huguenots and Englishmen

Apart from Jersey and Guernsey immigrants, Helier accepted a few French Huguenot refugees, among them

Cosmé Brévint, who became the first minister and schoolmaster, and surgeon Jean Quesle, with his wife Remy, whose midwifery was to be in frequent demand by a rapidly-growing community. English settlers numbered William Smith, the butcher and brewer; landscape gardener Jasper Dare, who gave his name to La Jaspellerie, and Thomas Roo, a jack-of-all-trades known as Thomas Le Faiseur.

A Fief Haubert

Hard-working colonists soon transformed the long-neglected island into a prosperous farming community. By 1571 the population had grown to about 200 and the windmill was built to grind their rich crops of corn. Farming tithes were making Helier wealthy and in 1572 he contentedly reported to Queen Elizabeth that Sark's defences were secure and the terms of her Letters Patent successfully achieved. The grateful Queen made Sark a Fief Haubert in its own right and sent Helier six cannon from the Tower of London, with ammunition and gunpowder. Henceforward, the seigneur owed homage to the sovereign in person and had to supply, if required, a horseman with 'haubert' (coat of mail) and complete knight's armour.

BID FOR INDEPENDENCE

As Helier's time was divided between his St Ouen and Sark fiefs, many responsibilities for the latter devolved on his eldest son and heir, Philippe. Two years before Helier's death in 1581, a general assembly of Sark people met with Philippe at Le Manoir to establish a full-scale court of law and legislature. This type of meeting was not restricted to the landowning tenants until 1605.

Philippe's brother-in-law, Eduoard de Carteret, was sworn in as bailiff and there were twelve elected jurats, a procureur, sergent de l'epée, sergent ordinaire, connétable, centenier, two vingteniers and two assistants—twenty-two officers for a population only ten times that size!

The ambitious Sarkese, taking Jersey as their model, aimed to replace the small fief court, which Helier had been empowered to set up, with a wholly independent administration. Helier, consistently ignoring requests to attend Guernsey's own Court of Chief Pleas, was behind the move to break away from the bailiwick of which Sark had long been part.

Sark's Chief Pleas met for the first time on 5 November 1579. Its recorded business was brief: an ordinance that pigs must be ringed to prevent damage to neighbours' property; anyone failing to do so, after due warning, would be fined six shillings.

As the Royal Court of Guernsey was then involved in a dispute with the Governor, Sir Thomas Leighton, Sark's declaration of independent intent went unchallenged for a time. But Guernsey could clearly not let little Sark get away with it indefinitely, especially at the instance of a Jerseyman. Guernsey's internal troubles having been resolved with the appointment as bailiff of Leighton's nephew, Thomas Wigmore, he was put in charge of a landing party on 30 May, 1582 with four jurats, the Crown Officers and, ominously, forty armed men.

Helier de Carteret had died in the previous autumn and been succeeded as seigneur by Philippe, who then worsened relations with Guernsey by claiming Norman law exempted him from paying *première saisine*. He was in Jersey when the Guernseymen arrived in Sark and they were met by his deputy and cousin, Philip Messervy. Wigmore ordered him to muster Sark's defence force. Fewer than the required *quarantaine* having assembled, Wigmore declared the island forfeit to the Crown, arresting his Sark counterpart, Edouard de Carteret, and two of the jurats.

Found guilty of usurping the Royal Court's authority, Edouard was imprisoned in Castle Cornet and, even after his release later that year, was never allowed to return to Sark. The Guernsey take-over was not wholly successful, however. Alerted by a petition from his tenants ('Greeting, Grace and Peace through our only Saviour Jesus Christ. My Lord, we, trusting upon such hope of good and convenient remedies. . .') Sir Philippe de Carteret appealed to the Privy Council. Their order in Council of 24 April, 1583 and the findings of a subsequent commission gave a compromise solution.

Philippe's position as seigneur was confirmed and his payment of *première saisine* reduced, but his request for a Seal to establish Sark's independence was refused. Guernsey's legal supremacy over Sark was also confirmed, but Sark gained the right to its own court, with five jurats, the senior one acting as judge. The new court would be established by Guernsey, but the people of Sark would elect the jurats. The offices of greffier, prévôt, connétable and vingtenier were approved; the first two, as now, 'appointed with the consent of the Lord of Serk', the others 'chosen by the inhabitants'.

It was another eleven years before the new court was set up, after Philippe's death and succession by his two-year-old son, also Philippe, for whom an uncle, Amice de Carteret, acted until he came of age. The ceremony took place in Sark on 16 July, 1594, before Sir Thomas Leighton and four Guernsey jurats. Robert Slowley, the English tenant of Grand Dixcart, became *juge* (judge).

Leighton then initiated a long alliance with the de Carterets. Amice later became the witch-hunting bailiff of Guernsey, a position he held for thirty years (1601-31).

RELIGIOUS CONTROVERSIES

Sark's faith was austerely Presbyterian, with services held in private houses until, early in the seventeenth century, they moved to a barn-like building known as the Temple; it was unheated, dimly lit, the thatch its only roof, the seigneur's its only enclosed pew. It still stands halfway along the line of cottages at right angles to Le Manoir.

The fifth synod of Channel Islands Presbyterian ministers was held in Sark during 1570, the year in which pastor Cosmé Brévint began the church register by recording that two children of Thomas Hamon, tenant of La Valette de haut, had been baptised.

Brévint made his own, unsuccessful bid for ecclesiastical independence, by not attending Guernsey convocations of his church. Earlier described as 'a true servant of God, hating vice and of excellence both in his life and his doctrine', short-tempered Cosmé was to lose the support of his flock, who called on their church's Guernsey colloquy to discipline him. Like the de Carterets, they had recognised the superior authority of the larger island. Spiritually and temporally Sark had bowed to *force majeure*.

Brévint died in 1605 and was followed, seven years later, by his son, Elie. The notebooks of Elie Brévint, discovered in a loft at Le Manoir two centuries later, provide much information on island affairs during his sixty-two years ministry. He tenaciously retained Sark as a Presbyterian stronghold and only after his death did it finally conform, at least verbally, to the Anglican Church, the last of the Channel Islands to do so.

Even as late as 1874, however, Cachemaille wrote:

With only three or four exceptions, all who have filled the office of Minister of Sark, including the present Vicar [himself], have come from France or Switzerland, have received their education at continental Universities or Colleges, and have been first consecrated to the ministry according to Presbyterian forms . . . Once settled at Sark they conformed *in greater or less degree* [author's italics] to the rites of the Church of England.

THE HARBOUR

Better communication with the world outside, or at least with Jersey and Guernsey, had been ensured in 1588, when the first boats sailed from Creux Harbour. Facilities in the early years of colonisation, with their need for heavy imports of raw materials, had been almost exclusively limited to the old landing place at L'Eperquerie. Goods had to be hauled up the cliff path on crude sledges, a form of transport still used in living memory, or on the backs of pack animals and their drivers.

After considering several sites, Helier de Carteret decided the best alternative to L'Eperquerie would be the Baie de la Motte, halfway down the east coast. As the bay was landlocked, a tunnel had to be cut from Chaussée Chenchannée to the north, where a road could be built up the rising valley to La Collenette.

The work was completed seven years after Helier's death. The harbour had no breakwater and was open to the southeast, while boats had to be hauled by capstan out of the reach of waves that surged in when the wind was coming from Jersey.

NEW LETTERS PATENT

King James I granted the Seigneur of Sark his seal in 1611 and approved new Letters Patent. These had a dual purpose: to ordain that anyone born outside Sark and wishing to live there should take an oath of allegiance to the Crown, and to halt the breaking up of the forty tenements by sale or divided inheritance, a process begun as original colonists died or moved away. Due to the King's Patent not being registered by the Sark greffier, this royal command was not enforced until after the English Civil War, which itself speeded the process of fragmentation.

BREAK IN THE SEIGNORY

The years of the Commonwealth interrupted the de Carteret seignory of Sark. Their sympathies were royalist, the island's apparently parliamentarian. In the summer of 1643, parliament stripped Sir Philippe, then under siege in Jersey's Elizabeth Castle, of his seignories at both St Ouen and in Sark. He died a few weeks later, but his son—another Philippe, who was to become Sark's fourth seigneur—held out in Mont Orgeuil Castle. He was freed later that year, when a naval force under his cousin, Captain George Carteret, regained Jersey for the Crown.

Within a few months the de Carterets had equipped a hundred men in four boats to attempt the recapture of Sark and its revenues. Describing the unsuccessful attempt, Brévint's notebook refers to Philippe as 'commonly called (during his father's lifetime) the "Monsieur of Serk" ', adding that 'God delivered the island' from his attack. Brévint obviously wanted no restoration either of the king or the family who had paid for his education and given him the Sark living.

An important home industry at that period was the knitting of stockings and the heavy pullovers known as 'guernseys'. War left these workers without money, raw materials or an outlet for their goods. To help them, parliament made an annual grant to Guernsey and Sark of 4lb of wool per head of population, while the Guernsey States decreed that none should be dispossessed for debt.

Expelled from Jersey in 1651 by the Commonwealth forces, Philippe de Carteret moved to France, where he fitted out privateers to harry English shipping. He left Sark in peace, however, and the island was run, to their own financial benefit, by the Le Gros family who held the offices of judge, prévôt and one jurat. They acted in close concert with Brévint, whose daughter, Anne, married the prévôt. Le

Gros property deals further splintered the tenements and Helier's *quarantaine* looked in danger of being doubled.

THE RESTORATION

Charles II's accession to the throne at the Restoration in 1660 brought the return of Sir Philippe's fiefs. He died three years later and was succeeded by his thirteen-year-old son, yet another Philippe.

On coming of age in 1671, young de Carteret turned his active attention to an accumulation of problems, religious and secular. Sark was still defying the Act of Uniformity by remaining obstinately Presbyterian. When Brévint died at the age of eighty-eight in 1674, Philippe appointed in his place Moïse Benoist, a Frenchman ordained into the Church of England by the Bishop of Winchester, whose diocesan authority the island now reluctantly acknowledged.

The officers of the Sark Court refused to accept Anglican rites, however, and on 19 May, 1675 Sir Philippe obtained from Charles II a patent which had the convenient side-effect of loosening the Le Gros grip on island affairs. It stated:

> . . . the Jurats having refused to take the oaths, and subscribe the declaration, and receive the Sacrament of the Lord's Supper, as directed by law . . . the Court of Guernsey having taken from them the civil authority; and whereas the rest of the inhabitants of Sark are poor and illiterate, or so averse to the laws of the Church of England as to be incapable of becoming Magistrates of the Said Island. The King orders and directs the Court of Guernsey to give oath to a Sénéchal and establish such other officers, Sheriff and Registrar, as shall be requisite for the administration of civil justice, and who shall be named by the said Philippe de Carteret.

So the people of Sark lost their hard-won right to elect jurats and the court reverted to its original fief status.

There was an ironic sequel to the last Sir Philippe's partially successful legal battle to stop the fragmentation of tenements by enforcing the Letters Patent of 1611, which had been belatedly registered in 1680. Impoverished as a result of his support for the Catholic King James, after the latter's decisive defeat by William of Orange at the Battle of the Boyne in 1690, the seigneur, then long absent from Sark, himself sold two parcels of land on Le Manoir estate— Clos de Messervy (La Hèche) and Clos de la Corderie. He also obtained royal consent to alienate the entire fief, but the projected sale fell through and he leased the island for three years to a Jerseyman, Daniel Valpy. Before that time was up, Sir Philippe had died.

The last two de Carteret seigneurs, Sir Charles (1693-1715) and Lord John Carteret (1715-20) did nothing for Sark. Charles's time was spent at the English court and he mortgaged his Sark property to Guernsey businessmen; John sold six further parcels of land and eventually the fief itself, having never once set foot in the Channel Islands.

All the de Carterets had to some extent been absentee landlords, but the last years of their 165 as lords of Sark were in sad contrast to Helier's pioneering zeal. It was believed that Lord John's agent decamped with the proceeds of the sale of Sark to a Colonel John Johnson; if true, the story probably gave wry satisfaction to the 'poor, illiterate, incapable' Sarkese.

9   YEARS OF CHANGE

'Not one family in Sark . . .
understands English.'
Adam Clarke, 1787

THE LE PELLEY FIEF

COLONEL Johnson died in 1723 and his executors sold the fief for £5,000 to James Milner; seven years later he too was dead. Neither of these English seigneurs left any mark on the island's history. Milner's executor, the Bishop of Gloucester, let the seignory go for only £3,700 to widowed Susanne Le Pelley, daughter of former Sark *juge*, Jean Le Gros. The last Sir Philippe de Carteret, who spent much time and money trying to loosen the Le Gros grip on Sark property and affairs, must have shifted uneasily in his grave.

The Le Pelley fortunes came from privateering, the officially licensed first cousin to piracy. With smuggling ('free' or 'fair' trading), this formed the most lucrative occupation for enterprising Channel Islanders from the seventeenth century to the end of the wars with France in 1815. Sark seafarers were involved in both activities, as they had earlier been with the islands' fishing fleets that sailed to Newfoundland. It may have been from their foreign contacts that smallpox reached Sark, causing major outbreaks in 1695, 1705 and 1731. Privateering Sarkese killed in action included Isaac and Thomas Vaudin, Paul Guille and Thomas Le Masurier.

Dame Susanne died in 1733. Her son and successor, Nicolas, continued to live in the Le Gros home, La Perronerie, which became the seigneurie and underwent extensive alterations. Le Manoir was given to the minister and remained the vicarage until 1934. Among innovations at the new manor house was a stone colombier by which the Le Pelleys reasserted a seigneurial right to keep doves or pigeons.

Eight of the Le Pelleys held the fief of Sark. While Pierre, the fourth of them, was under age, his mother, Elizabeth, dismissed minister Pierre Levrier, locking him out of his church. For more than three years no services were held. After Pierre came of age in 1755, he invited a Guernsey rector across to conduct one, but the enraged Levrier burst into the old chapel where it was being held and halted the prayers by raising the Clameur de Haro.

Guernsey's Royal Court upheld Levrier's protest, because the seigneurial right to nominate ministers does not extend to their dismissal. But Pierre, prompted by his mother, ordered the prévôt and constables to evict the unfortunate parson from Sark , an action that apparently brought no legal reprisals.

The controversy hardly endeared the Le Pelleys to their vassals, most of whom supported Levrier. Other bitter disputes followed. Protesting against what they considered an unjust monopoly, rioting islanders set fire to the seigneurial windmill in 1797, after the tenant of La Forge, Thomas de Carteret, had built a mill on the Hog's Back (a pile of overgrown stones marks the site today) and been upheld by the Royal Court, on condition that he used it only for his own corn. Another 'pirate' mill was erected   in Little Sark, its   gaunt, creeper-clad ruins now a daymark for fishermen. Poorer islanders challenged the hated *corvée*, a law finally rescinded in 1951, which forced them to work unpaid for two days each year on the roads, or pay a sum in lieu.

Rise of Methodism

These revolts against feudal privilege coincided with the rise of the Wesleyan Methodist faith, introduced in 1789 by Jean de Quetteville, who preached reform in the home of Thomas Mollet, freeholder of Clos à Jaon. John Wesley had written his Alderney disciple, Adam Clarke, on 26 March 1787, asking, 'Is there nobody who speaks English in the island of Serk?' Clarke replied, 'There is not one family in Serk who understands English. If the people of that island had understood it, I should have visited them long since.'

The Methodist upsurge was anathema to the Anglicans, whose following declined sharply after the Levrier episode. 'The Ministers of Serk, during the greater part of the seignory of the Messieurs Le Pelley ,' commented Cachemaille, 'were little superior to their predecessors. We know that several of them were inferior to them . . . but at that time there was little religious life properly so called . . . The public houses were open the whole of Sunday except during the hours of divine service. There they danced, played cards and other games. Labour went on just the same on Sunday . . . the Seigneur himself set the example, and his case was so outrageous that one of the constables was obliged to give him a severe reprimand . . .'

In the early 1820s, minister Jean M. de Joux persuaded Chief Pleas to pass an ordinance prohibiting the sale of drink on Sunday and closing the taverns.

A later proposal by tenant Elie Guille to stop non-essential fieldwork on the Sabbath also took effect. In a bid to revive waning Anglican congregations, the church of St Peter was built on land donated by the seigneur. Half the pews were sold for between £5 and £15 to the tenants and entailed at an annual rental with their tenements. The other half were free—the pre-condition for a grant of £400 from the English Society for Building Churches. However, it was the humble Ebenezer Chapel, erected by the Wesleyans for £300 in 1796, on land given by illiterate Jean Vaudin, that continued to attract the working Sarkese.

The Napoleonic wars

During the Napoleonic wars, service in the Sark militia, previously confined to the forty men with muskets, had been extended to all males between sixteen and sixty. A visual telegraph maintained communications with Guernsey, Jersey and Alderney, and a constant guard was kept in watch-houses on the coast. A warning bell (*cloche*) was erected on a mound where the church later stood, to alert the island in the event of invasion.

The French made only two brief raids. On one nocturnal landing in Little Sark, finding the watchmen asleep, they loaded their boat with sheep and departed. Another landing party at L'Eperquerie captured several Sarkese and took them to France. Otherwise the wars left Sark virtually unscathed and the island fishermen found good markets among the crews of naval ships anchored in the Guernsey roads.

Schools

Educational facilities improved under the Le Pelley seignory. In 1829, the schoolroom next to the old church at Le Manoir was replaced by a new school near Clos à Jaon crossroads. This became the boys' school ten years or so later, when Seigneur Pierre Le Pelley had another built for girls opposite Le Manoir—'thinking it', as Cachemaille noted 'best to separate them from the boys, and give them an education more adapted to their sex and future occupations'. During the 1840s, English was made a compulsory subject at both schools. Old gravestones and bones, discovered when the foundations were dug for the girls' school, suggest that the site was that of a medieval cemetery; some of the stones can be seen at the side of the road in front of the school.

Le Pelley efforts to get a new prison approved in 1832, to replace the almost derelict jail next to the new church, were less successful.   Chief Pleas insisted that if the seigneur wanted a modern lock-up, he should pay for it.

MINING

All mining rights were granted to the seigneur by the 1565 charter. Rumours of rich copper and silver deposits came to nothing until 1833, when visiting mining engineer John Hunt found traces of copper at Creux à Pôt. In the following year Pierre Le Pelley, grandson of the man who evicted Levrier, granted a twenty-one-year concession to mine Sark and Brecqhou. It was vested in the newly floated Guernsey and Sark Mining Company, which issued 200 £5 shares; Hunt took up thirty, Le Pelley ten. The first party of miners from Cornwall started work at Le Pôt in 1835. Cachemaille, whose ministry began in that year, takes up the story:

> Much labour was spent upon it; good indications were constantly turning up, but no paying metal. In despair Mr Hunt most carefully examined all the cliffs at Little Sark, and discovered rich indications of a vein of silver and lead . . . a greater number of English miners were sent for, the Pôt was abandoned . . . and the works at Port Gorey were pushed on with redoubled activity. An experienced captain, John Prince, was placed at the head of the concern; a powerful steam pump was had over, and later a steam winch was added for clearing out the levels.
>
> An ore which was very rich in silver was then obtained, worth £600 the ton, but the quantity was small and the vein

continued very narrow . . . a tea and coffee service of pure silver from the Sark mines was kept prominently before the Guernsey public; the sight encouraged the shareholders and helped to urge forward the work. The mining population . . . amounted to 250 souls, including women and children. Between 70 and 80 Sarkese were employed on the works . . . Nearly all the English miners were domiciled in Little Sark, which swarmed with people . . .

There were four shafts above Port Gorey: Sark's Hope, Le Pelley's, Vivian's and Prince's. Other workings had been opened at Port és Saies, where miners had to be lowered down the cliff by ropes, but difficulty of access forced these to be abandoned.

Triple tragedy

On 1 March, 1839, with the mining operations at their height, Seigneur Le Pelley set off from L'Eperquerie for Guernsey with boatman Abraham de Carteret and his eighteen-year old son, also Abraham. Cachemaille, a close friend of the seigneur, went to see him off in a strong southerly gale:

Thinking that they would probably wait till the tide had slackened, I made up my mind to take leave of Mr Le Pelley . . . I hastened to ascend the cliff that I might follow the boat on her way. When half way up, I was amazed to see that the boat had already started, with its foresail up, going straight towards the Pointe du Nez, where the tide made a high white wall of foam . . . I trembled for the boat and climbed higher up, so as to see better how it would pass that wall of water . . . At this moment the boat entered the tide and immediately rose up almost perpendicularly. An instant after we saw its keel shining in the sun, and a few seconds afterwards boat and all had totally disappeared in the waves and nothing reappeared.

The boat's remains were picked up in the Channel by the Portsmouth trader, *Two Brothers,* and its sternpost was washed ashore on Brecqhou; but the three bodies were never found and a memorial tablet in the church carries the Apocalyptic prophesy, 'La mer rendra ses morts'. The experience was so traumatic for Cachemaille, his subsequent terror of the sea so great, that he never again left Sark for the remaining thirty-eight years of his life.

Mining losses

Ernest Le Pelley, who inherited the fief on his brother's death, watched the mining venture stagger from one disaster to the next. Ore raised from the eight galleries of the four shafts, one extending 200ft under the seabed, contained too little metal; promising veins dwindled and died, and new injections of capital were needed to instal more powerful pumps, as water seeped menacingly into the the workings. At times of storm, the miners could hear boulders rolling on the seabed, far above their crouching heads. To raise more money, Le Pelley took a £4,000 mortgage on his fief from wealthy Guernseyman, Jean Allaire. A piecework bonus was introduced to spur the miners to even greater efforts, but Sark's 'Hope' was fast proving a mirage.

Finally seawater burst through a collapsing gallery ceiling, drowning ten miners and flooding the only profitable part of the workings. An oft-repeated story claims that, on the same day in 1845, a cutter carrying ore worth between £10,000 and £12,000 struck a rock off Guernsey, sinking with all hands and its uninsured cargo. The name of the cutter is never given, however, and there is no reference to the wreck in the 1845 files of two Guernsey papers, *The Comet* and *The Star,* though others are reported.

A Guernsey authority on local shipping history, Eric W.Sharp, says, 'I have no record of any wreck of a Sark ore boat other than the schooner *Horatio,* that hit the Black Rock off St Sampson's while on her way to Bristol on 8 January, 1841. She was got off, repaired at St Sampson's and proceeded.' Even today many Sark people believe it was this apparently mythical wreck, not the flooded gallery and cumulative burden of debt, that killed off a doomed enterprise.

Reduced operations went on as most of the Cornishmen left Sark, either to return home or seek their fortunes in America. One who stayed was Thomas Remphrey, three of whose descendants still live in Sark. Wild nights at the tavern opened for miners by a Guernseyman called Taylor were over. By 1847, the mine workings were deserted, Ernest Le Pelley and many of his fellow shareholders ruined. More than £30,000 had been lost in this futile flirtation with industrial capitalism.

Ernest died a broken man two years later, aged forty-seven. His son, Peter Carey Le Pelley, could not meet interest payments on the mortgaged fief. In 1852 Jean Allaire's daughter, Marie, widow of Thomas Guérin Collings, foreclosed and paid less than £1,400 to become Dame of Sark, after the mortgage and its overdue interest had been deducted from the agreed purchase price of £6,000. Like the de Carterets, whose tenure lasted thirty-three years longer, the Le Pelleys ended their seignory of Sark in financial ruin.

EARLY TOURISM

One side-effect of the mining operations had been to draw curious sightseers from Guernsey and Jersey; several shops and hotels were opened to cater for them. A typical trip was that by the regular Plymouth trader, *Sir Francis Drake,* in May 1841, when a party of eight ladies and gentlemen embarked at St Peter Port with hampers of cold fowl, ham, beef, pies, French rolls, English cheese, fruits, wine, cognac and gin. They were joined in the Guernsey roads by many other excursionists, who had been ferried out in small boats.

The prettily modelled *Drake* hissed and smoked as she awaited departure, while the captain paid his attentions to the ladies and each new party was greeted by a lively tune from the fourteen-piece band of the First Militia Regiment on the quarterdeck.

While the elegantly dressed visitors were inspecting the Sark mines, a thunderstorm soaked them and they had to borrow an odd assortment of dry clothing from the owner of a hotel. His lower dining room was crowded by a party of thirty, while the élite were waited on upstairs by several footmen, with the band playing outside. Re-embarkation took two hours and the vessel arrived back in Guernsey at 9 pm, the passengers, a contemporary account assures us, declaring themselves 'delighted with the day'.

Cachemaille was less enthusiastic. 'Sark', he declared with a heartcry that was to become perennial, 'was greatly altered. Tranquillity, monotony, solitude . . . all these were now far away.'

The mining collapse seems to have soured the usually cheerful Sarkese and visitors had a less friendly reception for some years afterwards. In July 1851, for instance, the *Princess Royal* was roughly received by fishermen waiting to ferry ashore its 170 passengers, when some of them tried to use the ship's own boats. Lady Carnarvon and family, and Admiral Jenkinson and his party, jostled as they landed, said they were 'greatly disgusted with the rudeness and insults . . . characteristic of an island of savages'. Shades of Rabelais!

Eighty excursionists on the *Sir Francis Drake* had a worse time in May 1853, when they attempted to disembark in

Guernsey boats that had crossed with them, instead of using the Sark fishermen's craft. Oars, boathooks and tillers were wielded to bloody effect, some ladies fainted, but eventually the determined visitors fought their way ashore. In the evening they found the harbour tunnel blocked by horses, oxen and carts—and had to force their way *off* the island. The day's outing had cost five shillings: 3s for the trip, 2s for landing and embarking in Sark. The Sarkese, not unnaturally, regarded the latter fee as theirs by right.

Cutters ran trips up to 1860, when the *Rover* offered a half-crown (12$\frac{1}{2}$p) return fare, leaving Guernsey on Wednesday, returning Sunday. The *Rival* of Sark, master Thomas Carré, made the crossing two or three times daily from 15 May to 15 September when the wind was eastward, but only five times a week when it was in the west. In August 1859 the Weymouth packet steamer, *Cygnet,* took 300 passengers on a round trip—Weymouth, Guernsey, Sark, Guernsey, Alderney, Guernsey, Weymouth. During the 1870s, encouraged by Seigneur Collings, Sark had between 4,000 and 5,000 visitors yearly.

A REVEREND SEIGNEUR

The Rev. William Thomas Collings, a Somerset curate and not, as Dame Sibyl believed, Canon of Wells, inherited the fief when his mother, Dame Marie, died soon after acquiring it, reputedly with Jean Allaire's proceeds of privateering. Most of her father's fortune, however, probably came from outright piracy. Guernseymen said he hoisted the French flag as a blind, when robbing and sometimes sinking British ships—and John Oxenham obviously modelled pirate Torode on him for *Carette of Sark.* Allaire's great-great-granddaughter, Dame Sibyl, considered him 'guilty of an unchristian temper, debauchery and iniquity', a character of a vastly different cut to his clerical grandson.

Like the Le Pelleys, Collings used Sark as his summer residence, appointing Cachemaille deputy seigneur when he moved to Guernsey's more sociable atmosphere for the winter. He spent much thought and money improving the island's tourist attractions—for instance, by blasting the Window in the Rock look-out above Port du Moulin. New hotels were built: Dixcart on its present site and the Victoria (later Bel Air) at the Collenette.

Collings bought the tenement of L'Ecluse, adjoining La Seigneurie and, with La Moinerie de haut, which the Le Pelleys had purchased, and the former seigneurie at Le Manoir, had a considerable estate and four votes in Chief Pleas.

End of the militia

He took great interest in the Royal Sark Militia, holding the rank of lieutenant-colonel and continually parading his hundred troops for drill and target practice. In 1859, with a red carpet laid at Creux Harbour, he and his militiamen were lined up to welcome the first visit of a reigning British sovereign. An unfavourable groundswell turned the royal yacht, with Queen Victoria aboard, back to Jersey, speeded by a salute from the loyal Sark guns. It was to be another hundred years before a queen of England stepped ashore.

The militia gradually went into decline—perhaps due to the seigneur's waning interest in later life; it had virtually disappeared in 1880 and was struck off the Army List in 1900.

An improved harbour

La Motte bay had remained without a breakwater until 1822, despite unsuccessful attempts in 1788 and 1816 to build one that would withstand the seas. In 1866, however, the wall was breached and Chief Pleas debated whether Creux should be abandoned and a new harbour built at L'Eperquerie. This move was favoured by Collings, but when it was decided to rebuild Creux, he helped to push the project through, particularly when a loan of £3,200 had to be raised towards the total cost of £6,000. The installations included a much stronger breakwater, wider quay and proper landing steps, with an opening to the north (since filled in), allowing water to escape and prevent surge when heavy seas were running.

Losses at sea

While the harbour works were in progress, Agnew Giffard, the engineer-in-charge, set off on an October evening in 1868 for Guernsey from Havre Gosselin in an 18ft gig. With him were his brother Walter; Russell Renouf, keeper of the breakwater lighthouse; medical officer, Dr Gatehouse, who was about to take up practice in Alderney, and J. G. Pilcher, a London oil merchant. 'They were told it was dangerous to go and that night would overtake them,' recalled Cachemaille. 'The tide carried them a long way to the south and the wind blowing from the north rapidly freshened until it became a regular tempest. The night fell and suddenly became intensely dark. The Sarkese . . . prophesised they could hardly escape death'.

The islanders proved right. The wrecked gig was found seven miles from Diélette on the Cotentin; Agnew Giffard's body at Havre Gosselin; his brother's at L'Eperquerie; Renouf's in the Gouliot caves, and two months later, Pilcher's at Niton, Isle of Wight, his skull and hands bare of flesh, but the clothing still intact and identification made by a breastpin bearing his father's likeness. The doctor's body was never recovered. A granite memorial erected by Pilcher's widow points its warning finger skyward on the cliffs above Havre Gosselin.

Four years later, the seigneur, with his wife, son and servants, narrowly escaped drowning during their November return to Guernsey for the winter. The steam tug *Gosforth*, which Collings had chartered, hit Petit Creux rock.

The passengers and crew, ten in all, eventually landed on Herm after two hours in a dinghy built for no more than six. The skipper, whose comment when the ship struck had been a despairing 'All's lost, all's lost', appears also to have 'lost his presence of mind', according to the account of the seigneur, who took command of the rescue operation. The Collings' luggage, which went down with the ship, contained Queen Elizabeth's original Letters Patent. They were not recovered, but two years later a case of books and family silver was washed up on the coast of Jutland. Identified by Collings's name still legible in the books, the property was reclaimed by his son, who was fortuitously visiting Denmark at the time.

The two wrecks reinforced Cachemaille's terror of the sea, which had been tragically justified earlier in 1872, when his son Eugène was lost in command of the *Ariel;* the ship sailed from London for Sydney never to be heard of again. Cachemaille died in 1877 after spending and chronicling forty-two years as vicar of Sark. A new pulpit, dedicated to his memory, replaced the old three-decker.

THE 'VIOLENT TERROR'

Collings survived Cachemaille by five years, during which he donated a chancel to the church, where the old high pews gave way to new ones. His seignory had brought many improvements to Sark, in addition to the prison that he persuaded Chief Pleas to have built in 1856 and the new graveyard on land given by him. In the year of his death, 1882, the Guernsey ketch *Cheval de Troie* began regular shipments of coal, which gradually replaced Sark's traditional fuel of furze and blackthorn.

Rev Collings's son and heir, William Frederick, was to prove a very different seigneur. Described by one of the Sarkese who still remember him as 'a violent terror when he had taken drink', he was heavily built, 6ft 4in tall, and had a temper that could be measured by the colour of his trouser cloth: white was set fair, blue forecast squalls. Some of the latter days are recalled in local court records and newspaper files.

Under the heading 'Alleged Shooting at Fishermen by the Seigneur of Serk' the *Jersey Press* (30 June, 1891) reported that Collings, then visiting Rozel, Jersey, in his yacht, had threatened to shoot the first fisherman daring to leave the harbour. Two of them attempted to do so, 'on which the Seigneur fired a pistol shot, compelling them to relinquish their intention'. By the time a constable arrived 'Mr Collings had left the harbour, but not before cutting several fishing boats adrift'.

On 18 June, 1892 he was brought before Sark Court on the complaints of J. Drillot, for seizing him by the throat and beating him; Thomas de Carteret, for having broken into his home with a pistol in his hand; and Philip Le Feuvre, for smashing two window panes at his house. He agreed to have the window repaired, was fined two livres tournois for the de Carteret offence and sent for trial in Guernsey on the Drillot count.

In July 1894 he was again conducted to Guernsey by the prévôt, after leaving the seneschal's court in contempt when brought before it for setting loose and threatening to kill two dogs belonging to a visitor—fined £5 or four weeks in jail.

Back to Guernsey the following July for having 'insulted, threatened and struck D. Robin, Constable of Serk, throwing his hat on the ground and calling him coward, damn fool and brute and also, during a previous case . . . making a false declaration under oath against Robin'— fined £5 or four weeks' imprisonment and bound over in the sum of £20 to keep the peace for a year, under the threat of a further month in jail.

He was before the Sark court in 1897 for firing his gun on the public highway at night. In 1903 he made two appearances, the first for having jostled the vicar, the Rev Seichan with his horse and striking him on the shoulder with a stick; the second for 'having brutally threatened Mrs Seichan with his stick, causing her injury and terrifying her to the point where she took refuge in the Bel Air Hotel and spent the night there'. Find on both counts, he was ordered to keep the peace with Mrs Seichan and all British subjects— a warning without effect. Violently anti-clerical, he feuded with Seichan until the end of the latter's ministry in 1922, even allegedly chalking slogans against him on the now-demolished kiln near the harbour (see Plates 10 and 11).

Well-matched eccentrics

At 6ft 6in, Corsican Seichan was even taller than the seigneur. He had been chaplain on Devil's Island when Dreyfus was imprisoned there; he left the Roman Catholic faith to marry an English Protestant, but conducted services with High Church ritual that infuriated the Calvinist Sarkese, many of whom joined the Methodists. His politics, like his Christian names, Louis Napoleon, were Bonapartist. With a black cloak flung flamboyantly over the left shoulder, he affected the kind of hat popular in Paris before the Franco-Prussian war.

Seichan sued Collings for £140 damages in 1902, claiming the seigneur had grossly libelled him in a letter to the Bishop of Winchester. In 1908 there was litigation about a tombstone erected, without the vicar's consent, over the grave of tenant William Baker's father. The stone had been overturned by an enraged Seichan and, though the tenant was granted legal right to replace it, the vicar's physical presence was so intimidating that it lay where it had fallen until he departed fourteen years later.

Seichen and Collings were well-matched eccentrics, the vicar high-handedly authoritarian, the seigneur reflecting an arrogance of power without responsibility not untypical of landowning gentry at that time.

In 1912 Collings was before the Guernsey court charged, reported *The Star* (19 September) 'with threatening to shoot Mr G. Lovibond and using threats towards his daughter Miss Doris Collings on 29 August, 1912 on the White Rock (Guernsey)'. He had been under restraint for a fortnight while mentally examined and Dr Robinson, who had seen him six times, reported he was 'in full possession of his memory and perfectly sane'. The charges were proved and the seigneur had to give bail of £50 as guarantee of good conduct for twelve months.

At the ordinary court that followed, Dudley Beaumont applied, on behalf of his wife and her sister Doris, 'to see his relatives appoint a guardian to the seigneur on account of his intemperance, prodigality, disordered conduct and mental weakness'.

THE ENGLISH INVASION

Apart from colourful language and behaviour, Collings contributed little to Sark at a time of transition. During his seignory some beautiful houses disappeared, like that of the Godfray family, demolished to make way for Stock's Hotel. The Beauregard tenement house, gutted by fire in 1892, was rebuilt as another hotel. There were improvements in communications, with regular postal deliveries replacing the haphazard arrival of mail on any available boat, to be carried up Harbour Hill in a wicker washing basket and dumped for collection in de Carteret's store at La Collinette. A postal telegraph link with Guernsey opened in 1903, though public phone calls were not available until 1918. At Havre Gosselin, a jetty built in 1912 saved passengers the hair-raising climb on an overhanging iron ladder, when easterlies closed Creux.

A two-mile-long procession celebrated King Edward VII's Coronation in 1902. All the islanders and visitors took part, so there were no spectators, and long-silent guns on the headlands fired a loyal salute.

To expanding tourism was added the arrival of tax-avoiding English settlers, who began to buy out Sarkese tenants, or obtain long leases from them to build new houses. Before the turn of the century, two tenements, La Fripponerie and La Jaspellerie, left local hands never to return. By 1920 they had been joined by La Rade, Clos de Menage, Clos de la Ville and La Forge, with more to follow. Sir Hilgrove Turner, Jersey's attorney general, built La Vermandée; other new immigrant houses included Le Petit Champ, La Chaumière, St Magloire and Le Chalêt. One attempt to buy into Sark happily failed, when Collings rejected a £30,000 offer for his fief from Horatio Bottomley, later the notorious swindler, who intended to open a casino.

A declining birthrate—6.4 annually in 1926-30, compared with 17.6 in 1875-80—reflected the replacement of young Sarkese by ageing outsiders and the toll of World War I. Seventeen men of Sark—five Guilles, three Carrés and two de Carterets among them—died, most of them in a unit of the Royal Guernsey Light Infantry decimated by one withering German barrage. The whole inter-related island was plunged into mourning overnight.

Peace brought pressure for democratic reforms from a majority that had been deprived of its voice in communal affairs since Chief Pleas became limited to landowning tenants in 1605. Trevor Blakemore and others helped the poor farmers and fishermen to frame proposals—eventually approved in Privy Council as the Sark Reform Law of 1922—that included the election to Chief Pleas by adult suffrage of twelve People's Deputies. They abolished plural voting, and the seigneur's right to veto legislation was limited by granting Chief Pleas' right of appeal to the Royal Court.

This split Sark into three antagonistic camps: Radicals opposed to any change; Moderates prepared to

Plate 25 La Coupée in 1902, two years after railings were first erected *(John Morton)*

Plate 26 On the headland opposite Tintageu, with Brecqhou behind *(John Morton)*

Plate 27 Grand Autelet through the man-made Window in the Rock and *Plate 28* natural arch in Port du Moulin from the north *(John Morton)*

Plate 29 Grève de la Ville cave and *Plate 30* La Grande Moie through a natural arch in the same bay *(John Morton)*

Plate 31 Rocky outcrops at Les Fontaines bay in Little Sark

Plate 32 The spirit of Sark, whose 'people work if they choose'. Left to right, the late Jenette Hamon, Winter Vibert and Tom Baker *(M. P. Joyner)*

countenance minor alterations, and the Third Party of reform. The radical majority in Chief Pleas filibustered and mauled the eventual projet de loi so badly that Guernsey's Lieutenant-Governor, Sir John Capper, came over with his retinue to tell them the island's administration would be forcibly taken over unless they agreed to changes approved in Privy Council.

The 1920s had their lighter side. Among several army officer immigrants was Captain Ernest Platt, who organised an annual regatta, with races for swimmers, scullers, motor boats, and, once, even dogs. Platt also offered a prize for the first person to swim from Guernsey to Sark. Impossible, said local fishermen, but John Hayward did it in 1927, taking 4hr 55min to reach Vermandaie. In that same summer, Seigneur William Frederick Collings died at the age of 75, a sadly muted shadow of his old, bellicose self.

10   DAME SIBYL'S ERA

'It was time to bring them up
at a good, round turn.'
Dame Sibyl Hathaway

ORN in January 1884, the elder of Seigneur Collings's
two daughters, Sibyl Mary Collings was later to
describe her father as 'extremely insubordinate, madly
obstinate, fiercely self-opinionated and prone to outbursts of
ungovernable rage', but also 'a generous man and a
wonderful companion'. Her childhood was shadowed by
having one leg $2^1/_2$ in shorter than the other, a handicap she
overcame to become a proficient cliff-climber.

As soon as she could hold a gun, her father taught her to
become a scourge of Sark rabbits. She rode a succession of
donkeys, one of which stubbornly refused to cross La
Coupée; she loved swimming and loathed sea travel. That
echo of Cachemaille dated from her teens, when the *Alert*,
in which she was crossing to Guernsey, stalled in a gale off
Jethou and drifted among the rocks until towed to St Peter
Port.

At seventeen she and Dudley Beaumont made a runaway
marriage at St James's, Piccadilly; her father had thrown her
out of La Seigneurie at midnight, in her nightgown, when
told of her intention to wed. In England she spoke for the
ultra-patriotic National Service League, but returned to
Sark in 1912, settling at La Valette de bas with her husband
and breeding pedigree Guernseys.

In World War I she was a VAD nurse in London. Beaumont, having served in France and Africa, died in 1918 from Spanish 'flu; she was at that time expecting Jehanne, the seventh of their children, four boys and three girls. One boy, Basil Ian, died in infancy. Afterwards she worked with the British Army of Occupation in Germany, learning the language she was to find useful in reversed circumstances twenty years later.

DAME OF SARK

In 1927, on the death of her father, with whom she had by then become reconciled, Dame Sibyl returned to Sark, taking her seat in Chief Pleas at a special meeting called soon after the funeral. The main business was to sack the medical officer, who had arrived in her father's sickroom a week or two earlier carrying a forked stick, which, he said, was for killing snakes. This same eccentric had a previous brush with authority in the mid-1920s, when he brought over the first motor car to be seen in Sark. After it had been driven up Harbour Hill, the doctor was taken to court, fined and warned that, if he wanted to use it again, the car must be drawn by a horse.

Like her grandfather seventy-four years earlier, Dame Sibyl found La Seigneurie in a state of shabby neglect, undecorated for twenty years, still without a bathroom or water tap. She sold Allaire's home and other property in Guernsey to help pay for renovations.

Within her first year as Dame, Mrs Beaumont became engaged to a Sark newcomer, 'Major' James. Vicar Ernest Greenhow refused to marry them, recognising James as a man whose wedding he had conducted in Singapore seven years earlier. Soon afterwards James decamped with several hundred pounds given him by Dame Sibyl to pay renovation bills in Guernsey. On 2 July 1928 Douglas James, aged forty-five, was sentenced to three years' penal servitude at the

Central Criminal Court for frauds committed over many years.

A year later Dame Sibyl met and married in London Robert Hathaway, who was American-born, but had become a naturalised Briton since leaving the United States in a one-man protest against their prohibition laws. As seigneur, Hathaway shared his wife's responsibilities and became extremely popular with the Sarkese.

THE 1930S

Visitors to Sark came over from Guernsey in the steamships *Riduna*, *New Fawn* and *Courier*, with the motor vessels *Joybell I, II and III*, while those from Jersey arrived in the SS *Brittany*. *Joybell I* was the former Margate lifeboat; *Joybell II* sank outside Creux, her propeller being recovered when it surfaced nearly forty years later, while *Joybell III* started life as the tug *Albert Edward*. The last of the old paddleboats, *Helper*, irreverently known as 'God Help 'er', had been pensioned off.

In these pre-war years Sark grew its own grain and there were plenty of fishing boats. Their blue-guernseyed owners, solid men like Bill Hamon, John Henry and 'Boss Eye' Pippard, rolled up Harbour Hill, with their catches strapped on their shoulders in wooden boxes, and stopped off at the Bel Air, raising nightly echoes with 'Alouette', 'Auprès de ma Blonde' and the rest of the island repertoire.

At Easter, Bel Air staged Sark's liveliest dance as climax to the annual soccer tournament. On one Bank Holiday, probably 1934, when the boats offered an excursion return ticket for one shilling from Guernsey, more than 1,000 people crossed. There were four football teams: Sark United, The Rest, Juniors and Buffs. United, with baker Hubert Lanyon in goal, wore black and amber; The Rest's goalkeeper was Dame Sibyl's youngest son, Richard Vivian 'Tuppenny' Beaumont, with Dave Adams another member of the side. Dave had arrived from Wiltshire, where he was a stable lad, met Bill Hamon's daughter, Maude, at one of the dances, married her and became the island builder.

Artists' colony

Another soccer star was author and artist Mervyn Peake, who set his strangely disturbing novel, *Mr Pye,* in Sark of that period. His later trilogy, *Titus Groan, Gormenghast* and *Titus Alone,* carried strong echoes of the island he loved and his illustrations for these and other books included many well-known Sark faces.

Painters had been drawn to Sark since the eighteenth century when Joshua Gosselin, a Guernsey naturalist and descendant of the Beauregard Gosselins, came to execute detailed water-colours and draw an early geological map. Turner and Paul Naftel captured the wild beauty of the cliffs; William A. Toplis bridged the nineteenth and twentieth centuries, remaining doyen of Sark's artists until World War II. There was Arthur Bradbury, who later painted Dame Sibyl's portrait and built a studio in Rue du Moulin; Ethel Cheeswright, who spent 74 of her 103 years on Sark and died in 1977; Mr and Mrs Arthur Waller and their daughter, Margaret; Rowland Wheelwright, usually accompanied by one of the glamorous models who adorned his pictures of Venus Pool or the Fairy Grotto; Ann Jay, who married artist-hotelier Tom Sutcliffe after the war, Tony Bridges, who became a London vicar; Captain Lindsay Garrard and many more.

Mervyn Peake first came to Sark in 1935, on the invitation of his former art master at Eltham College, Eric Drake. With his wife, Drake had built The Gallery, to show the colony's work—and neighbours complained about wild, Bohemian parties. The Gallery is now the post office and general store.

Improved facilities

The Island Hall—built in 1928, on land given by Dame Sibyl, and financed by Captain E. G. Marden and family—had among its attractions, as listed by the 1934 *Sark Guide:* 'A large Entertainment Hall, a Miniature Rifle Range, Skittle Alley, Games Rooms and a full-sized Billiard Table . . . a safety Cinema, a Wireless Installation and a very fine Magic Lantern. Books and papers are available. The whole building is lit by electricity and is centrally heated.'

Privately generated power was the exception, not the rule on the island. An advertisement boasted that Stock's was the 'only Hotel in Sark with electric light,' a claim contested by the Dixcart announcement of 'Electric Light throughout'—which also added: 'Favourite Residence of HRH the late Prince Henry of Battenberg and of the late Victor Hugo'.

The Sark Pharmacy, then in Rue Lucas near the old post office, offered 'celebrated Sark Honey Suckle Perfume and Eau de Cologne—Specialities manufactured on the Island.'

Since 1927 there had been talk of a new harbour to supplement Creux, which dries out and can take passenger or cargo boats only from half-tide up to half-tide down. At other times there was the delay of transferring visitors to rowing boats and ferrying them ashore from outside the harbour, while south-easterly winds put it out of commission. Opinion was divided between making Creux a deep-water, all-weather harbour with five berths, at an estimated cost of £38,000, or—for £45,000—constructing an entirely new jetty further north. After lengthy and heated opposition, which many feel has since proved well founded, the more expensive choice was made.

The site was north of Chaussée Chenchannée and to reach it a tunnel had to be blasted through Pointe Cagnons into Maseline bay. Work began in 1938 and, by the time it was halted by the war, the tunnel was complete and the first stump of jetty pointed towards the lighthouse. Plans included a bridge across the gully south of the tunnel, but a storm shattered it and the gap was subsequently filled in.

Aspects of pre-war life

The contract with the harbour construction company stipulated that no Sark person working for them would be forced to join a trade union. Unions and closed shops, like cars, income tax and political parties, are not welcome in Sark, During the 1930s, however, Dame Sibyl, at least, seemed unworried by aircraft noise. Lord Sempill and others visited La Seigneurie by plane; she crossed from Guernsey in a Puss Moth, and 'Tuppenny' Beaumont, an aircraft amateur, touched down on Sark to bring a petrol-laden whiff of the speed-crazy, Hollywood-slanted world outside.

During 1938 Clifford Maclagen, Mary Lawson and others arrived to star in *Toilers of the Sea,* a filmed version of Victor Hugo's novel, written during his Guernsey exile (1855-70), when he was a frequent Sark visitor. The set transformed Creux Harbour into the St Sampson's waterfront of the early 1800s and Les Autelets replaced the Roches Douvres for the wreck of the *Durande.* Sark fishermen did well on the day rate for extras, but the film was never screened. The company, in which Dame Sibyl's heir-apparent, Lionel 'Buster' Beaumont, had taken a financial interest, collapsed. He left Sark with the cast, never to return; while on RAF leave during the war, he died in a German air raid on Liverpool.

The church had been passing through a trying period. The Rev R. H. Phillips was inducted by the Dean of Guernsey in April 1938 as Sark's fifth vicar in five years—a sriking contrast with the sixty-three-year incumbency of Elie Brévint and Cachemaille's forty-two-years. 'Stop your quarrelling, bickering and nonsense,' was the theme of the Dean's admonitory sermon; while the *Guernsey Weekly Press* commented: 'Were it not controlled by a system of law and retribution, this multi-vicar complex in the inhabitants might in time even lead them (rashly, we think) to cast an incumbent bodily forth.'

Two bungalows went up for sale by auction in May 1938. Bidding started at £50 and stuck at £75; both were withdrawn as the reserve price—£115 for one of them—was not reached. At the same sale a pony cart fetched 5s (25p); in 1939 the schoolmaster's salary was raised from £70 to £100 a year.

OCCUPATION

The first winter of war gave little warning of what lay ahead. It was business as usual in 1940 when the English visitors started to arrive in Sark, lulled by Home Secretary Sir John Anderson's assurance that no restrictions would be imposed on summer travel to the Channel Islands. By early June the north-eastern sky was darkened by the blowing up of oil-storage tanks by the French at Cherbourg and boatloads of terrified refugees from France were calling at Creux Harbour, where the islanders, notably baker Lanyon, provided them with food.

Other frightened people were ferried to England in thousands from Jersey, Guernsey and Alderney. Some residents, including the doctor, left Sark; the rest, all the Sarkese among them, took the example and advice of the seigneur and dame, deciding to face a now inevitable German occupation.

On 28 June, twenty-eight people were killed by bombs and machine-gun fire from Heinkel planes in St Peter Port; Sark fishing boats were sprayed with bullets, luckily without casualties, as the aircraft flew back to France. Four days later an advance party of German officers landed and were received at La Seigneurie by the Hathaways.

Determined to assert her position, Dame Sibyl took the dominant role in negotiations. 'My name and status were included in the *Almanach de Gotha,'* she recalls in her autobiography—a trump card, she considered, in 'dealing with upper-class Germans'. Throughout the five long years of occupation she insisted on going to the top authority when trouble threatened and she established a friendly relationship with several aristocratic members of the Wehrmacht, notably Baron von und zu Aufsess and Prince Oettingen, whom she visited in their German homes after the war. Her story of those years was dramatised by William Douglas-Home, with her permission, in *The Dame of Sark* and produced at Oxford and in London's West End a few months after her death.

The first two years of German presence passed quietly, apart from the forced landing of a Lancaster bomber near La Seigneurie during the 1941-2 winter. Inevitably there was fraternisation—in soccer matches between the occupiers and occupied, or at dances and other social events. Otherwise the Sarkese busied themselves growing food and catching fish.

COMMANDO RAIDS

Then, in September 1942, eleven British residents were listed for deportation; among them were a middle-aged couple who attempted suicide—the man succeeded, his wife eventually recovered. A month later, two Germans were killed in a British Commando raid. Mrs Frances Pittard, widow of a former medical officer, helped the raiders with information when they broke into La Jaspellerie; a broken pane of glass led German investigators to her. She was jailed for a time in Guernsey, released, but later deported to a prison camp.

Relations were no longer so friendly. The curfew was extended. More than 13,000 mines ringed the beaches and cliffs, cutting off access to furze and blackthorn that were once more being used for fuel, and to vraic again serving as manure. Even the cemetery was mined.

A bigger group of deportees departed to prison camps in January 1943, among them Seigneur Hathaway, a Guille family of ten and a Hamon family of nine. The deported Sarkese seem to have been named at random; those still living on the island can offer no explanation why they were chosen. Bob Hathaway, a natural and courageous anti-Nazi resister, was to be as popular with fellow-detainees at Laufen Camp as he had been with the Sarkese, though the experience destroyed his already failing health. He died in 1954, five weeks after he and Dame Sibyl celebrated their silver wedding.

News of the progress of the war reached Sark through BBC broadcasts; the islanders' radios were mostly improvised crystal sets, kept in defiance of the German ban. Another source of Allied information was *GUNS* (Guernsey Underground News Service), distributed in Sark by Hubert Lanyon, helped for a time by Cyril Wakley and the Methodist minister. The Guernsey publishers were caught, two of them being sentenced to fifteen years' imprisonment. Lanyon, identified by an unwise entry in a Guernsey diary, had two teeth knocked out by German interrogators, but bravely refused to name his helpers. He escaped with a six-month sentence, reduced to four on appeal. Dave Adams, working as a diver in Guernsey, made an unsuccessful, and fortunately undetected, attempt to blow up a German escort vessel.

Commandos again raided Sark at Christmas 1943. This time the casualties were French-Canadian members of a landing party who failed to cross Pointe Derrible, then ignored briefing instructions by following the trail of their 1942 predecessors up the Hog's Back. Two were killed by exploding mines; the others, one badly wounded, escaped the way they had come. A dance at the Hall that night had been attended by Christmas-celebrating Sarkese and

German soldiers—there was still some social contact.

The Channel Islands were bypassed when the Allied invasion moved into Normandy in 1944, leaving 30,000 German soldiers on Jersey, Guernsey, Alderney and Sark in a pocket of isolation. The islanders had to wait what seemed a never-ending year for liberation. Food grew steadily shorter. The Sarkese were eventually helped by the arrival of Red Cross parcels, while the Germans, forbidden to touch a three-month emergency supply of food stored against a siege, began starving to death.

Sark owed much to Mrs Annie Rebenstorff, widow of a German-born, naturalised Belgian, who came to live on the island in the 1920s. 'Mrs Reb' usually managed to forage food and other essentials for those who needed them most. She died in 1958 and the affectionate nickname, 'Mother of Sark', is on her gravestone.

News came through on the radios on 8 May, 1945 that the Germans had surrendered. That night a huge bonfire, topped by an ancient carriage belonging to Charlie Perrée, blazed on the north-west coast and there was dancing at the Hall. When British troops arrived, it was to collect the German arms and pile them in Rose Cottage; they put Dame Sibyl in command and, almost incredibly, departed for several days, leaving some 275 enemy soldiers at large. Only a locked door barred their way to guns with which they could have killed everyone. In fact two of them died clearing mines in Creux Harbour.

The forty muskets had already gone. Those relics of a half-forgotten defence force, and other firearms, had been taken from the hooks on farmhouse rafters five years earlier, handed to the Germans and smashed in a pit at the Bel Air, their HQ until a faulty oil heater exploded and burned it down. The present hotel of that name is 100yd away, on the other side of Harbour Hill. The Bungalow Hotel in Little Sark had gone, too. Some of the other bungalows and most of the trees had been sacrificed as fuel. But Sark escaped the fury of destruction elsewhere and there was only one new name for the war memorial.

As throughout occupied Europe, bitter accusations were made of collaboration, informing and thefts from temporarily unoccupied property. But the scenes in nearby Normandy, where girls who had been over-friendly with the Germans had their heads shaved in public, were not repeated in Sark. A popular German medical orderly, Werner Rang, had a warm welcome when he returned to settle on the island with Phyllis Baker, a Sark girl he had married in England.

A fictional film of wartime Sark, *Appointment with Venus,* starring David Niven and Glynis Johns, was shot in 1951, giving work to Sarkese extras. It has become a hardy annual for summer film shows; at least its views of the cliffs are authentic.

POSTWAR CHANGES

The island soon recovered from its four-year occupation, and work resumed on Maseline Harbour which was eventually completed at a war-inflated cost of £65,000. But even feudal Sark could not escape the winds of post-war social change. It is surprising, in retrospect, that so few alterations were made with a firebrand like Henry Head about. Guernseyman Head was married to Florence Emily Le Feuvre, tenant of La Ville Roussel de bas and, by proxy, occupied her seat in Chief Pleas. A sharp thorn in the side of the establishment, having studied and understood the laws better than most, he was known as 'the stormy petrel'. Many of his proposals had the backing of Deputy Lanyon and they initiated the island's second Reform Law of 1951.

The seigneurial veto was finally replaced with a delaying process of twenty-one days for reconsideration of proposals opposed by Dame Sibyl and her successors. Elections of deputies were put on a clear, three-yearly basis and it was ordered that properly audited accounts should be submitted to each New Year meeting of Chief Pleas.

The tenants retained three-quarters of the voting strength, though absenteeism sometimes led to their being outnumbered by deputies. This brought a rebuke from Seneschal William Baker that work was being left to the deputies—and a semi-serious suggestion from Hubert Lanyon that Chief Pleas should be replaced by an elected assembly of twenty.

Meetings were particularly stormy in the 1950s. Head and Lanyon had been members of a Land Reform Committee, elected by Chief Pleas to establish whether it was possible, under feudal law, for native Sarkese to buy small plots for building. They claimed to have found many unauthorised alterations to tenement boundaries, some made during the present century.

In 1958 they called for a Royal Commission to investigate irregularities in the island administration, a proposal that found little support and provoked a letter of protest, signed by 148 Sark persons, to the *Guernsey Evening Press*. Many of the points they raised have since been rectified.

QUATERCENTENARY—AND AFTER

Sark celebrated the 400th anniversary of her Elizabethan charter in August 1965. Despite all the pressures, its feudal structure was largely intact and, appropriately, Guy Malet de Carteret, Seigneur of St Ouen in Jersey, was among those honouring the quatercentenary.

The rash of shanties that had erupted to join those of the 1930s finally resulted in Chief Pleas electing a natural amenities committee; but comprehensive development proposals, commissioned from and submitted by planning expert G.A. Jellicoe, were thrown out by fifteen votes to twelve in 1968.

Some curb on building had become inevitable, however, and it finally came in a 1974 projet de loi halting the erection of new dwellings for three consecutive periods of eight months—two years in all—with the exception of work already approved and applications from established Sark residents. The move was proposed by Dame Sibyl as a stopgap measure, pending long-term legislation to discourage wealthy immigrants. An ironic side-effect was to boost property prices to a level only the very rich could afford—one stone-built, three-bedroom house being advertised at £90,000 in November 1974.

The 'Great Abdication'

An earlier crisis earned 1969 the title 'Year of the Great Abdication', when Dame Sibyl threatened to hand her fief back to the Crown. Several disputes in a long hot summer of discontent had split Sark into hostile factions and, at eighty-five, Dame Sibyl decided 'It was time to bring them up at a good, round turn.' A bluff? 'Not at all,' she said, 'Sark had to learn to deal with things more seriously, either with me or without.' She believed the Privy Council would have asked Guernsey to take over Sark's administration, a move neither island wanted. Predictably things went her way! During the same year, popular Seneschal Baker was not re-appointed at the end of his eighth three-year term. In his place Dame Sibyl named Bernard G. Jones, a Guernsey bank official.

End of the era

Dame Sibyl was a remarkable woman, autocratic but with a keen sense of humour and, to the end of her long life, an acute intelligence. Some of her views were eccentrically unorthodox, like the reply she made to a suggestion that immigration of English workers had been beneficial by reducing inter-marriage among the closely-related Sarkese: 'In-breeding is no problem if you start with good stock and it has never been a problem with our old Sark families. It's when you go outside and import stock about which you know nothing that the trouble can start.'

Much of her leisure was spent entertaining English residents at bridge parties, but she complained that outsiders were running Sark's business life. She attributed the declining number of Sarkese to families being smaller than in her youth, not to young islanders moving elsewhere.

Dame Sibyl lectured extensively abroad to attract more visitors, but at the end realised Sark might be sacrificing its birthright of unspoiled beauty for a mess of tourist pottage. Three months before her death she admitted tourism had reached saturation point, but she sponsored what amounted to a tractor-drawn bus service up Harbour Hill, a move pre-war Sark would have regarded with incredulity and horror.

Her son-in-law, Harry Bell, deputy seneschal for ten postwar years and deputy seigneur after her death, summed up Sark's feelings at her passing in 14 July, 1974: 'Whatever else happens this is the end of an era.'

Ten years later, to mark the centenary of her birth, Guernsey Post Office made a special issue of five stamps. They showed her as a girl of 16, with the Seigneurie in the background (9p); receiving, with Bob Hathaway, two German officers at the 1940 occupation (13p); with the Queen and Prince Philip in Sark, on the 1957 Royal visit (26p); as an old lady (28p); and, with a backdrop of the Seigneurie gardens, the rose that bears her name, *Dame of Sark* (31p).

11   A DYNAMIC COMMUNITY?

'. . . wondrous happy isle
That troubles not its sleep with future care.'
Trevor Blakemore

SEIGNEUR BEAUMONT

WITH the death of Dame Sibyl, Sark again had a seigneur, her grandson John Michael Beaumont, then aged forty-six. For the first time, the succession of the seignory had leapfrogged a generation, as a result of Lionel Beaumont's wartime death.

Born in Egypt, where his father was on RAF duty, Michael Beaumont had become a design engineer in aerodynamics, a career far removed from life in feudal Sark. With his wife Diana and two teenage sons, he faced a complete change from the provincial environment of red-brick Bristol and his working world of guided missiles. They all, however, had the advantage of knowing the island from holiday visits and Diana Beaumont is a daughter of former deputy John La Trobe-Bateman, whose mother came to Sark in World War I.

The new seigneur's first appearance in Chief Pleas was at the 1974 Michaelmas meeting, a few weeks after his grandmother's death. Seneschal Jones paid tribute to 'Dame Sibyl Hathaway, honoured by her Sovereign when made a Dame Commander of the Most Excellent Order of the British Empire in 1965', before the assembly stood in silent memory of a remarkable old lady, not universally loved, perhaps, but certainly respected by everyone who had contact with her. Dame of Sark for as long as most of those

144

present could remember, she had seemed almost indestructible, providing for them a welcome link with past security and a symbol of continuity—like island blacksmith John Hamon carrying on his grandfather's trade and teaching son Trevor to follow him.

The Seigneur's inaugural speech helped reassure those who distrusted his technological background: 'We are a dynamic community in a changing world and it is inevitable that we will, as we have done in the past, change and adapt to suit it . . . we have here in Sark a unique heritage of custom and law, envied by people the world over . . . controlled here in this court by what must surely be the most democratic institution in the world today . . . we have managed to maintain the beauty, tranquillity and peace in which we are fortunate enough to live and for which our visitors come to see us . . .'

Much of the business that followed was concerned with rising prices and the Seigneur's first administrative proposal, carried unanimously, brought all-round salary increases to the island's officials. For Sark, like the world outside, there was no escape from spiralling inflation.

At La Seigneurie, the butler and other staff were dismissed, only one gardener remaining to fight an uphill battle against invading weeds. In fact, when the Beaumonts took up residence in May 1975, it seemed the wheel had gone full circle for the seignory of Sark, as they prepared to turn the vinery into a tomato greenhouse, part of the grounds into a market garden, and eight rooms of the big house into two flats for letting during the holiday season. To survive as Sark's feudal ruler, with limited means in the economic climate of the 1970s, meant becoming the first working seigneur since Helier de Carteret. The Beaumonts had the blessing of the islanders—with some head-shaking scepticism about their chances of success.

SARK

Like his grandmother, Michael Beaumont believes the feudal system, relegated elsewhere to the history books, is still ideally suited to Sark's small community, where so much depends on voluntary work. He announced his intention to immerse himself in island affairs and Sark learned that the Seigneurie bridge parties had died with Dame Sibyl; he neither played nor, he said, was he 'a very sociable person'.

Housing restrictions

The greatest problem, in his early view, was to check permanently the building and purchase of property by outsiders . . . Sark must not become 'a tax retreat for the English or anyone else'. He favoured residential qualification for building houses, with restrictions on the purchase of properties and granting of 99-year leases, to prevent the Sarkese being bought off their own island. Coupled with the effects of the 1974 Finance Act, with which Westminster closed many Channel Island taxation loopholes, this made a discouraging prospect for wealthy, would-be settlers.

But it is not easy to find a happy medium between the 'pull up the gangplank, Jack, I'm on board' philosophy and Sark's previous open-door policy. Even if the former option could be socially acceptable, it was seventy years too late; to freeze the population in its present form, with an immigrant preponderance of elderly people, would invite slow suicide. Immigration, controlled only by the seigneurial right of refusing *congé*, on the other hand, had produced an equally unsatisfactory situation. Two things were clear: the 1974 ban on building had helped to push property prices out of reach for any but the wealthy, but if Sark continued to need permanent immigrant workers, it would, in fairness, have to let them put down residential roots.

For many, the restrictions were like the tractor legislation—a case of locking the stable door after fifty-seven machines (the 1975 level), had been driven through it.

While conceding that was correct, the new seigneur recognised a fact of Sark life, 'you need to go over the hump here, before anything can be done about it', and cited the amenities committee as a case in point—'a real monstrosity of a building had to go up before the idea of restrictive legislation could be accepted'. Eventually, his idea of a more permanent check came in legislation stipulating that new houses could be built only by those with a 15-year residential qualification.

Control of tourism

Sooner or later — and preferably sooner — Sark must also face up to the vast numbers of day visitors in high season and agree on a sensible ceiling. In 1990 some 75,000 adults paid the landing tax, a staggering increase of 25,000 on 1974. Add children and parties from private boats and the total figure would be nearer 95,000. The result: overcrowded roads, queues for the inadequate toilets, litter-strewn cliffs, beaches and fouled hedgerows. An attempt to curb the numbers in 1976, when they were far less, was overwhelmingly defeated.

Nobody wants day visitors barred, but there is a strong case for an economically viable quota, that can be comfortably and hygienically absorbed. Sark's enduring charm has been its peaceful remoteness and freedom from the excesses of the world outside. That charm is now in danger.

The Beaumont seignory has seen some welcome changes. Agriculture has shown encouraging signs of a renaissance. Sanitation has been greatly improved, with a treatment plant above Les Lâches rendering innocuous the raw sewage collected from cesspits, before discharging it into the sea; previously it was spread on fields as manure. Locally-quarried stone is again being used in building. And the Island's administration has been streamlined with the introduction of computers. The Water Carnival, revived in

1981, after a lapse of more than fifty years, is now a popular annual attraction.

An armed French invasion highlighted 1990. It was a one-man foray by André Jean-Pierre Gardes, who had made a reconnaisance visit in June. He returned on August 23 and, the following day, put up posters proclaiming that Sark was French and he the rightful seigneur. He patrolled Rue de la Seigneurie, brandishing a semi-automatic weapon. Disarmed by Constable Philip Perrée and overpowered with the assistance of others, Gardes was brought before the Seneschal's Court, deported to Guernsey and jailed for a few days. An attempt to return in 1991 failed.

Another who had disputed the Seignory of Sark, Dame Sibyl's estranged youngest son and only surviving child, Richard ('Tuppenny'), had died in England in the 1990 summer. In 1972 the Privy Council had rejected his petition that Dame Sibyl had no right to be Dame of Sark and that, *inter alia,* his nephew, Michael was the rightful seigneur. Ironically, two years later he was.

What of Sark's future? Seigneur Beaumont sees the threat of Channel Islands EC membership as a potential cloud: 'How long would the Common Market and its offshoots, like the Court of Human Rights, leave us alone?' he asks. 'Will Sark be forced into using EC-approved abattoirs? Will the prison be acceptable? Will a common tax law be introduced? Will our feudal land-holding be allowed to continue? Will the EC stand offshore finance?'

These are some of the questions worrying Islanders, notably those deriving substantial income from alternative company directorships, in what has become known in financial circles as the 'Sark Lark'.

'There will certainly,' believes Michael Beaumont, 'be pressure from the young in Guernsey and Jersey to join, as very soon they will not be eligible, as of right, to take jobs within the EC if we remain outside. Already locals have lost the right of abode in the UK.'

Its tiny size makes Sark especially vulnerable and the measure of the community's dynamism, paradoxically, may be in an ability to withstand changes that would irrevocably destroy its beauty in tranquillity. For the moment it remains an oasis of peaceful sanity—may that oasis never become a mirage.

BRECQHOU

'*Revenons chez nous, mon père,*
le monde est si mauvais."
A Brecqhou expatriate

SEPARATED from Sark by the 80yd (73m) of swirling Gouliot Passage, little Brecqhou is an island apart. Landing is by permission of the tenant and few Sarkese have ever set foot there. Its 160 acres (65ha) slope gently down westward for 1,200 yd (1,097m) from the 240 ft (73m) heights of Pointe Bélême to low cliffs bounded at the north-west by Moie Batarde, 20ft (6m) high, used as a mark by sailors and joined to the island only at low water.

The tableland, a mere 360yd (329m) wide, has one shallow depression to the north, sheltering the main buildings. The coast is heavily eroded from the north-east corner of La Haute Pêche and the little landing place at Galet de Jacob, Brecqhou's counterpart to Havre Gosselin, but used at low tide and when it blows strongly from the south-west. The steps of 'Jacob's Ladder' make a daunting climb to the clifftop, in contrast with the little harbour of Le Port bay to the south, where a road zigzags up from a recently re-metalled jetty, which dries out. The headlands and inlets of Creux à Cormorans, Pointe au Marinel, Bélême, Pointe à Fouille, Pointe du Port, Le Cagnon, Creux à Caper and Moie de la Quane to the east and south are in stark, impressive contrast to the west and north, where Moie Batarde is the only sizeable outcrop, Creux és Vaches the lone inlet.

Like its bigger neighbour, Brecqhou is ringed by rocks. To the south are Boue Batarde and Les Dents, showing their black stumps above low water, La Ray (skate), La Touraille (tower) and Le Cheval (horse); west lie Moie de Givaude, 43ft (13m) high with its offstanding Demies, and the shark-finned, treacherous Nesté, which dries 20ft (6m); to the north, Le Piquillon, Rocher Dève (burnt rock) below the big house and Boues du Poisson; east, Moie and Boue de Gouliot and, almost detached from the cliffs, the pyramid of Petit Bélême.

Several notable caverns include La Cave aux Pirates (pirates' cave), opening from an inlet to the south-east and easily recognised from the sea by its lofty entrance. Accessible only by boat, it penetrates deeply. Local lore says Brecqhou is honeycombed by a maze of caves, housing a colony of rats descended from ancestors that deserted a sinking ship in 1665, when its passengers were trying to escape the Bubonic plague raging in London. A narrow cleft at the inner end of Cave aux Pirates could lead to this unexplored labyrinth, if indeed it exists. More than a century ago Cachemaille reported 'an immense heap of cinders, the product of various kinds of combustibles' near the cleft, which could have been left by pirates or smugglers in earlier times.

GEOLOGY

There has been no geological survey in recent years, but a party organised by the Maritime Laboratory of Dinard paid a brief visit in August 1939, when Dr A.E. Mourant, of Jersey, reported most of Brecqhou to be granite 'seen in several spectacular sections overlying the schists, as it does in Sark. On both north and south coasts, about 400yd from Pointe Bélême, the main junction is seen to dip westwards, the granite thus lying both above and west of the schists. Two faults . . . bring the junction up again near Le Port . . .Two mica trap dykes, one on the north and one on the south coast, and three dolerite dykes were noted.' A quarry to the west yielded 'the freshest specimens anywhere of the Sark type of granite'. The party found several large blocks of a mineral vein, consisting of a fine-grained banded mixture of quartz and laemalite and, at Pointe à Fouille, some strikingly contorted schists containing a vein of quartz and white, coarse-cleared pyrites clearly visible from the sea.

The mineral blocks were almost certainly raised during Brecqhou's share in Sark's mining venture, though an unauthenticated story claims Dutchmen worked copper there much earlier. A shaft with a squared roof facing south-east was opened in the mid-1830s and a report to the mining company in 1838 stated: 'The present working lode has a very imposing and promising appearance near the sea. It contains plumbago and carbonate of lime, in which good yellow copper ore is found. A level has been driven west fifteen fathoms and the lode cut through from wall to wall, which is about 14ft, but it has not opened according to expectations.' Soon afterwards the workings were abandoned, because of constant flooding from underground springs.

Brecqhou has no shortage of underground water and there are three wells. One just below the swimming pool, on a lawned terrace north of the big house, is by the site of a fresh-water pond, now filled in; 10ft (3m) down the well lies a rich vein of amethystine Sarkstone quartz. About 30ft (9m) above mean sea level in the cliffs at Le Port is a fine example of raised beach, its sea-washed stones bared when the road was cut.

FLORA AND FAUNA

Brecqhou's most prolific form of animal life has long been the rabbit. Londoner F. Wearis, who had been living in Sark, wrote in 1675: 'Nature has provided us with a regular warren, placing at a small distance in the sea an island, of about half a mile every way over, which is inhabited by nothing else, whither we commonly go a ferreting, and have thence such abundance that . . . some families here have made £15 or £20 a year only of their skins.'

George Sharp, who farmed Brecqhou 1911-29, is reputed to have introduced Belgian hares, which interbred with the rabbits to produce a strong, healthy strain that had the sleekest pelts and finest flavour in the Channel Islands. The rabbits proved a pest to successive tenants, until they began to be decimated by myxomatosis in 1974.

English botanist Cecil P.Hurst, who spent a week on Brecqhou in 1902, found several flowering plants and a fern not recorded on Sark before or since. These included the Narrow-leaved Pepperwort (*Lepidium ruderale*), Small-flowered Melilot (*Melilotus indica*), Bush Vetch (*Vicia sepium*), Buckwheat (*Fagopyron esculentum*), two grasses and the Adder's Tongue fern (*Ophioglossum vulgatum*). The Sark check list of 1957 gave twenty-two species found only on Brecqhou and a list prepared for the late tenant in 1969 included 292 species. There is a wealth of wild flowers and in April the bluebell-carpeted cliffs mistily mirror those on Sark.

The exposed tableland does not favour trees and in 1902 there were only a few cultivated sallow willow bushes and tamarisks. Trees have been introduced more recently, with the sycamore and Austrian pine appearing to thrive .

LIFE ON BRECQHOU

Hurst described Brecqhou as 'in the happy position of being an island without a history '. Least written about of the Channel Islands, it is usually dismissed in a few lines as an adjunct of Sark, despite having great natural beauty, its own unspoiled charm and the finest views of Sark's glorious west coat. The Evodia (or Evoda) mentioned by Paulus Warnefridi (*c* AD 780) as the island where three French boats were wrecked may well have been Brecqhou, where the name survives as Givaude, although his reference has also been attributed to Alderney. Similarly, it is uncertain whether the Besargia of early medieval documents referred to Brecqhou or Little Sark. The modern name, sometimes spelt Brechou, derives from the Gothic, *brican* (gap) and *ou* (island), a clear allusion to the Gouliot Passage.

It was long known as Ile és Marchants, later corrupted to Ile aux (or des) Marchands (merchants' island), which inspired legends, perhaps coincidentally true, of pirates having stored stolen merchandise there. But the name came from the Guernsey family of Le Marchant, who acquired Brecqhou in 1363 by inheritance from Guillaume de Cheny, seigneur of Vinchelez in Jersey. Brecqhou was attached to his fief and, when Guillaume died, it was disjoined for his daughter, Jeanne, the wife of Denis Le Marchant. It still belonged to the family in 1563, when the Crown Commissioners' grant to Helier de Carteret of Sark 'with all the other isles adjacent to it' apparently ignored their claims.

The position was finally resolved in 1681, when Sir Philippe de Carteret brought an action in Guernsey's Royal Court against Rachel le Moigne, widow of James Le Marchant, who held power of attorney for their eldest son, Sir William Le Marchant. The claim was 'to see right done . . . concerning the Island of Brechou'. Dame Rachel surrendered her son's rights without awaiting judgement and public documents subsequently referred to the seigneurs as 'Lords of Sark and its dependencies'.

Apart from rabbiting, Brecqhou was used for grazing. In the late sixteenth century, three cows belonging to Guernseymen were stolen by English pirates, who also accosted a Sark boat returning from Guernsey, kidnapping crew member Jean Hotton; he later escaped and returned home.

Despite the fictional house featured in *Carette of Sark* during the Napoleonic wars, there is no evidence of any dwelling on Brecqhou before 1836. Seigneur Pierre Le Pelley then built the farmhouse, usually known as Dower House, to encourage cultivation by settling two Sark families. Early residents were named Amy and de Carteret. A father and daughter moved to Alderney, but after six weeks the girl pleaded to return home to Brecqhou, because 'le monde est si mauvais' (the world is so evil).

Inhabitants

There were five people on Brecqhou in 1845; census returns show it was deserted in 1851 and 1861, but there were five again in 1871 and a Guernsey family called Naftel lived there for five years from 1876, the 1881 population being given as seven. Apart from sheep grazed by the Bests of Guernsey, the island was said to be unoccupied for the next twenty years, although the 1891 census showed two residents, perhaps shepherds.

A married couple and their four children moved in for a five-year spell as caretakers in 1901; in the following year Hurst found three people working the land, with 60 acres under wheat, barley, oats, parsnips, beans and beetroot, some rough pasture and the rest covered with heather, gorse, bracken and brambles.

Deserted again from 1906-11, Brecqhou then enjoyed its longest continuous spell of habitation, when George Sharp arrived from Alderney with a sixty-year lease at £20 pa from the seigneur of Sark, a boatload of furniture, farming equipment and animals—which were lowered overboard to swim ashore. With him were three relatives and a carpenter. Plenty of work awaited them, clearing weeds and thistles 6ft high. Sharp later married diminutive Agnes Lanyon, schoolteacher and aunt of Sark's Hubert Lanyon. He farmed there until 1929, when Dame Sibyl sold Brecqhou for £3,000 to Angelo Clarke, a former hotelier who had been living in Guernsey for many years. 'My father had always wanted the island for his own little kingdom', Clarke's son told the *Daily Chronicle*.

Tenement rights

With Brecqhou, Clarke acquired a seat in Chief Pleas, Dame Sibyl transferring to him the rights belonging to her tenement of La Moinerie de haut and the tenancy has since carried automatic admission to the *quarantaine*. Angelo Clarke's stay was short-lived. After three years breeding dogs there, he sold Brecqhou to his Irish namesake, Captain Tom Clarke, fifty-one-year-old member of a Cork family whose fortune came from tobacco. When he met the agent, Clarke was wearing a filthy raincoat and proffered a cigarette case filled with half-smoked stubs; yet he bred pedigree horses, had a priceless collection of oriental china and owned a luxury yacht, the *Ancilla*.

His tenancy brought big changes in the 1930s, among them the palatial house, which cost £13,000 and netted its builder a profit of just £63. Centrally-heated, it has six bedrooms, each with its own bathroom; staff quarters with two bedrooms; a huge, oak-floored drawing room, study and library, dining room, butler's pantry, kitchen, refrigerator room and linen room.

Clarke had the jetty built at Le Port and an aerial cableway, or 'blondin', weighing 100 tons constructed by a firm of Aberdeen iron founders to carry cattle, furniture, and supplies. He also installed an electric generator, and fresh water from the wells went to overhead tanks, from which it would be gravity-fed to supply the house and irrigate the fields. A pump on the shore filled separate tanks with seawater to service the toilets.

Tom Clarke and his wife moved to Devon when war came and, later, to Mull, where he died in 1944. His art treasures remained on Brecqhou throughout the German occupation and, amazingly, nothing was looted or disturbed. A long, legal wrangle about death duties on Clarke's £300,000 estate ensued in the Dublin High Court and the big house stood empty, the island overgrown.

Squatters

Ex-army officer Edwin Lawton and his thirteen-year-old son paid several visits in May 1947, intending to exercise squatters' rights. Stormbound for a week, they lived on snared rabbits and gulls' eggs. Dame Sibyl sent the prévôt to warn them off and told fishermen not to charter their boats to Lawton. He made one more landing and was evicted by La Dame's bailiff, who tore down from the jetty a notice proclaiming, 'No person may land on this island without the permission of the undersigned, Edwin Lawton, Capt. of Brecqhou.'

A recluse

The warning foreshadowed Scottish textile magnate J. Thomson Donaldson, a recluse by inclination, who bought the tenancy later in 1947 and stayed until 1965, when he unexpectedly gave his staff a fortnight's notice and retired to Zurich. During much of his tenancy thirteen people lived on the island, including Charles and Ethel Talbot, a Jersey couple who looked after the farm. Everyone else was rigorously excluded and the farm manager did not repeat his one mistake of 1957, in allowing ashore a botanical research team.

A millionaire

Apart from a caretaker, Brecqhou had been deserted for a year when multi-millionaire Leonard Matchan landed for the first time in April 1966, went straight to the house with the agent and asked the price of the tenancy. He had taken the precaution of getting Dame Sibyl's *congé* to buy. The agent, quoting £125,000, said a firm of Birmingham property developers were interested. Matchan told him they had no chance with Dame Sibyl and offered £40,000. In the event he paid about £46,000, with farming equipment included.

Head of two merchant banks and an international complex of companies with an annual turnover near £100 million, Matchan had the City reputation of getting his own way. Cosmetics, mink farming, fashion, engineering, plastics, hotels, fruit machines, publishing, professional football and speedway were among areas in which he successfully involved himself, after starting life in a Fulham back street, the son of a sewing machine engineer.

Much of his business was conducted over a battery of telephones, and a Gazelle helicopter carried him to meetings in Jersey, London and Paris. The aircraft caused his one brush with Chief Pleas, when Sark residents complained of noise and a law was proposed to ban its use. Astute sieur Matchan announced he would insist on his own rights if the machine were grounded. Sark would have to maintain his roads, and the sixpence-a-tail bounty for rabbits clearly applied to Brecqhou, which had an estimated three million; Sark could have them all—at that price. He was promptly invited to rewrite the proposal and the helicopter was secured. He did not overfly Sark or land there, unless help was requested for taking over a vet, or lifting off a seriously ill person in bad weather.

When Channel Islands postal services were separated from the United Kingdom in 1969, Matchan proposed Sark should issue its own stamps, as he had done with six denominations (1d to 2s) for Brecqhou. A committee was elected to discuss the matter with Guernsey, but it was eventually forgotten during Dame Sibyl's threat to relinquish the fief. A new move in 1982 was dropped in favour of Sark getting $1^1/_2$% of Guernsey's PO profits. Guernsey paid Sark £4,233 in 1989, £5,000 in 1990.

The Matchan coat of arms—two seagulls, a wave and three trefoils—was incorporated for Brecqhou, with Dame Sibyl's permission, into Sark's adopted Norman standard with its two leopards *passant guardant* or on a cross of St George. Matchan and his charming companion, Sue Groves, brought many improvements to the little island. Ponies and donkeys were raised in neatly parcelled paddocks, six workers looked after things, provisioned partly by three cows, home-grown potatoes, beans, greenhouse tomatoes and other vegetables. Outside supplies arrived on a fast launch and an old Cornish fishing boat, that made regular trips from Guernsey.

Then, in 1984, Brecqhou was again on the market, an illustrated advertisement in *The Times* speaking of a 'Unique Private Channel Island Haven of Exquisite beauty and romance . . . fully equipped and operational as an independent entity.' It was later withdrawn. Sadly, Leonard Matchan was to spend the last years of his eventful life in a Jersey nursing home. He died in 1987, ensuring, he believed, that his companion, Sue's lease of Brecqhou would be secured for her lifetime by a trust he had established. Sark law decreed that his son, Peter, should inherit the tenancy and he is legally contesting Sue Groves' right to continue living on and running the island. If precedent is any guide, the case could last a very long time.

Meanwhile, the seclusion is complete. Brecqhou is well cared for, beautiful and, except by invitation, to be admired only from the distance.

APPENDIXES

A
SEIGNEURS OF SARK

1565-81	Helier de Carteret
1581-94	Philippe de Carteret (son)
1594-1642	Sir Philippe de Carteret (son)
1642-60	No seigneur during Commonwealth
1660-63	Sir Philippe de Carteret (ii; son)
1663-93	Sir Philippe de Carteret (iii; son)
1693-1715	Sir Charles de Carteret (son)
1715-20	Lord John Carteret (cousin)
1720-3	Col. John Johnson (by sale)
1723-30	James Milner (by sale)
1730	Bishop of Gloucester (as executor)
1730-3	Susanne Le Pelley (by sale)
1733-42	Nicolas Le Pelley (son)
1742 -52	Daniel Le Pelley (brother)
1752-78	Pierre Le Pelley (son)
1778-1820	Pierre Le Pelley (ii; son)
1820-39	Pierre Le Pelley (iii; son)
1839-49	Ernest Le Pelley (brother)
1849-52	Peter Carey Le Pelley (son)
1852-53	Marie Collings (by sale)
1853-82	Rev. William Thomas Collings (son)
1881-1927	William Frederick Collings (son)
1927-74	Sibyl Mary Beaumont (Hathaway from 1929; daughter; with Robert Hathaway as seigneur, 1929-54)
1974	John Michael Beaumont (grandson)

B
TENEMENTS AND TENANTS

	1565	1991
GREAT SARK		
Aval du Creux	Nicolas Cristin	Edward Alexander Ian Robson

GREAT SARK	1565	1991
Le Carrefour	Clement Hacquoil	Mrs Louisa Baker
Clos Bourel	Edouard Gregory	Miss Molly Joanna Bull
Clos de Dixcart	Jean Noel	Mr and Mrs John Cubbon
Clos de Menage	Jacques Dolbel	Julian Neil Llewellyn Palmer
Clos de la Ville	Philippe Alexandre	John Mount Stephen
La Collenette	Lucas Le Masurier	Donald Vernon Willis
Dosdâne	Nicolas Guille	Edric Baker
L'Ecluse	Jean Le Cerf	Miss Beatrice Caroline Bell
La Forge	Regny Le Quedy	Rossford de Carteret
Le Fort	Pierre Rogier	Mrs June Carré
La Friponnerie	Julien de Carteret	Miss Jenny Allen
La Genetière	Jean Guille	Jamie Ross Guille
Le Grand Beauregard	Nicolas Gosselin	William Falle
Le Grand Dixcart	William Smith	Percy George Woolford
Le Grand Fort	Jean Le Brocq	Edward Charles Perrée
Le Jaspellerie	Edouard Brayer	Jonathan Charles Brannam
La Moinerie	Hiou de Carteret	Mrs Heather Lily Baker
La Perronerie	Isaac Le Gros	John Michael Beaumont
Le Petit Beauregard	Noel Vaudin	Mrs Florida Perrée
Le Petit Dixcart	Pierre Le Brocq	Mrs Patricia Falle
Pomme de Chien	Robert Jagault	Christopher Rang (Retraite)
Le Port à la Jument	Nicolas Du Val	Mrs Dorothy Lucien Mesny
La Rade	Jean Vibert	John Henry Jackson
La Rondellerie	Guillaume Chevalier	Alan Marsden
La Seigneurie	Helier de Carteret	John Michael Beaumont
La Tour	François Le Couteur	Dennis Hurden
La Valette de bas	Jehannet Hotton	Mrs Katherine Miller and Andrew Miller
La Valette de haut	Thomas Hamon	Mrs Henrietta M. Carré
La Vaurocque	*Benjamin Poindestre	Trevor R. Donnelly
Le Vieux Port	Guillaume Tanquerel	Ensor Baker
La Ville Farm	Jean Quesle	Mrs Gwendoline Drawmer
La Ville Roussel	Richard Poindestre	Peter Miller
La Ville Roussel de bas	Pierre Le Feuvre	Colin Francis John Guille (Retraite)
LITTLE SARK		
La Donnellerie	Gregoire Warre	Mrs Iris Williams
La Duvallerie	Jean de Carteret	Mrs Esther Perrée

APPENDIXES

GREAT SARK	1565	1991
La Moserie	Raulin Vaudin	Philip Perrée
La Pipeterie	Colin Pipet	Philip Perrée
La Sablonnerie	Jean Nicolle	Elizabeth Perrée

BRECQHOU

†La Moinerie de haut   Thomas Paychin   Peter Matchan

  * First recorded tenant, *c* 1580. Thomas Poindestre may have been first tenant.
  † Formerly in Greak Sark; seat in Chief Pleas granted to tenant of Brecqhou in 1929.

C
THE ADMINISTRATORS

SENECHALS

1675	Pierre Gibault	1841	Philippe Guille
1680	Thomas de Beauvoir	1851	Thomas Godfray
1683	Philippe Dumaresq	1876	William de Carteret
1702	Jean Payne	1881	Abraham Baker
1707	Philippe de Carteret	1891	Thomas Godfray
1744	Henri de Carteret	1920	Thomas Campbell
1752	Pierre Le Masurier	1922	Ashby Taylor
1777	Henri Le Masurier	1925	Frederick de Carteret
1785	Amice Le Couteur	1937	William Carré
1808	Jean Le Couteur	1945	William Baker
1812	Jean Falle	1969	Bernard G. Jones
1830	Elie Le Masurier	1978	Hilary Carré
		1985	Laurence de Carteret

GREFFIERS

1675	Thomas Machon	1830	Philippe Tanquerel
1703	Philippe de Carteret	1837	William Robert
1707	Jean Esnouf	1855	Jean Vaudin
1734	Pierre Le Masurier	1891	Joseph Mollet
1752	Henri Le Masurier	1898	Philippe Carré
1784	Thomas de Carteret	1927	Phillip Thomas Carré
1812	Thomas Godfray jnr	1951	Hilary Carré
1819	Elie Le Masurier	1978	John Hamon

TREASURERS

1978	Michael Terry	1991	Trevor Hamon

PRÉVOTS
(no complete record appears to have been kept)

1594	Noel Vaudin	1871	Hirzel Baker
1660	Jean Le Gros	1920	Alfred Baker
1741	Robert Slowley	1934	John Baker
1819	Thomas Godfray	1938	Philip Guille
1855	Thomas Le Masurier	1968	John Guille
		1980	Alfred Adams

D
THE SERCQAIS PATOIS

This short glossary records some of the unwritten Norman French patois of Sark, now spoken by only a few score of the islanders after surviving in a pure form with later additions, for more than four centuries (see p 56). The spelling, which can be only approximate, is based on normal French pronunciation, but the terminal 't' is generally sounded and a long vowel has been denoted by a circumflex accent (eg *pirôt*, goose, is pronounced pee-rote).

English	Sercqais	French
after you	aprie teu	après vous
afternoon	a'shtarlevèe	après-midi
always	tréjoue	toujours
argue	s'emateu	disputer
banker	l'bantyi	le banquier
barley	l'bleie	l'orge
basket	l'paunyi	le pannier
bat (animal)	la côt-souris	la chauve-souris
bean	l'pi d'mai	le haricot
bed	l'liet	le lit
bird	l'oueseu	l'oiseau
blacksmith	l'forgeu	le forgeron
break (v)	d'pichi	casser
brush (n)	l'brouaise	la brosse
bucket	l'boutiet	le seau
carpenter	l'tierpenti	le charpentier
ceiling	l'céelin	le plafond
cemetery	la chimtire	le cimetière
chair	la tiaire	la chaise
chest (body)	l'estouma	la poitrine
chicken	l'pouechein	le poulet
child	l'ésfant	l'enfant
cliff	la banque	la falaise
coal	l'tierbon	le charbon
come here!	vétan ichin!	venez ici!
corn (cereal)	l'formen	le froment
cough (v)	toutre	tousser
cow	la vacque	la vache
cowardice	co'ouar	lâcheté
dark	niet	sombre
dawn	o'jeu	le point du jour

163

APPENDIXES

English	Sercqais	French
deaf	oui'dur	sourd
ditch (n)	l'canneu	le fossé
do you know?	savou'en?	savez-vous?
dog (n)	l'tchon	le chien
door	l'lû	la porte
doorframe	la case d'lû	la chambranle
dress (n)	l'frôc	la robe
dungheap	l'mai	le fumier
dying	i's'meurt	mourant
ear	l'ourelle, l'oui	l'oreille
evening	o'sair	le soir
eye	l'yi	l'oeil
face (n)	la fache	le visage
farmcart	l'terriôt	la charrette
father	l'poière	le père
finger (n)	l'deu	le doigt
fireplace	l'graie	le foyer
fish (v)	poietyi	pêcher
flour	la flieu	la farine
fly (n)	la môque	la mouche
follow me!	sui'meu!	suivez-moi!
foot	l'pi	le pied
fork (n)	la forque	la fourche
furrow	l'rye	le sillon
glad	benaise	heureux (se)
goat	la biche	la chèvre
goodbye	à buèto, à la prechen	à bientôt, au revoir
go out	dehaleu	sortir
goose	l'pirôt	l'oie
gorse	l'jaon	l'ajonc
grasshopper	l'critiet	la sauterelle
grave (n)	la fôse	la tombe
greedy	glioton	gourmand
guillemot	l'gaude, l'autiette	le guillemot de troie
hair	l'g'veue	le cheveu
happy	i'est fi	heureux(se)
hedge (n)	l'fosset	la haie
hedge sparrow	l'verdaleu	la fauvette d'hiver
herring gull	l'mauve	le goéland argenté
Herm (island)	Herp	Herm
hide (v)	s'muchi	cacher
hip	l'tchisse	la cuisse

English	Sercqais	French
horse	l'g'va	la cheval
house sparrow	l'grosbec	le moineau domestique
isn't it hot	qui chaleu!	quelle chaleur!
jackdaw	la cahouette	le choucas
jacket	l'corset	le veston
Jersey (island)	Jerri	Jersey
jug	l'môgue	le pot, la cruche
kettle	la caudire	la bouilloire
key	l'cliet	la clé
king	l'rouai	le roi
kiss (v)	boiesi	embrasser
kitchen	la tuisainne	la cuisine
knit	ouvreu	tricoter
lamb	l'annié	l'agneau
lazy person	l'nivloteu	le fainéant
leave (v)	tyiteu	quitter
leather	l'tuir	le cuir
leg	la gambe	la jambe
light (n)	la veue	la lumière
lightning	l'épar	l'éclair
loft	l'solyi	le grenier
mackerel	l'mactié	le maquereau
make use of	s'jevi	se servir
manor	l'monnyi	le manoir
manure	d'conreu	le fumier
match (n)	l'brisqui	l'allumette
more	pus	plus
mother	la moière	la mère
move on!	sha!	marchez! allez-vous-en!
neddle	l'epile	l'aiguille
next	prechen	prochain(e)
no	naunin	non
old	vi	vieux, vieille
one	iun	un
overcoat	l'gran-cotte	le pardessus
oystercatcher	l'pie marange	l'huîtrier pie
painter	l'dessineu	le peintre
pencil	l'pinciau	le crayon

APPENDIXES

English	Sercqais	French
pig	l'couechon	le cochon
pillow	l't'yisin	l'oreiller
plenty	touplain	bien assez
plough (n)	la tierrue	la charrue
plough (v)	cacheu	labourer avec une charrue
pocket (n)	la paute	la poche
quiet	trantille	tranquille
razor	l'razeu	le rasoir
razorbill	l'barbelote	le petit pingouin
right	dêtre	droit
sad	tristre	triste
Sark	Ser, Saire	Sercque
saucer	l'sauci	la soucoupe
saucepan	l'saspain	la casserole
seaweed	l'vraic	l'algue
shirt	la qu'minse	la chemise
shop (n)	la shoppe	le magasin
short of breath	l'haleine montée	hors d'haleine
skirt	l'skirt	la jupe
slowly	douchement	lentement
snow (n)	l'nef	la neige
south	suc	sud
sou'west wind	vent d'servaie	vent du sud'ouest
spit (v)	écopi	cracher
spread (v)	épeni	étendre
stamp butter (v)	peinteu l'bure	empreindre le beurre
stomach	l'cor	le ventre
storm (n)	l'temps rudre	l'orage
tack (with boat)	boudinyi	louvoyer
take away	agrapineu	arracher
talk (v)	i'd'vise	parler
teapot	l'pôt à teie	la théière
their	l'ute	leur
three	trye	trois
thumb (n)	la pochi	le pouce
time	l'côp	le temps
toe	l'orté	l'orteil
too much	bel et bain	trop
tree	l'orme	l'arbre

166

English	Serqais	French
trousers	les briais	le pantalon
very	i'en dur	très
warm	cau	chaud
water	l'ieau	l'eau
wave	la pièche de mier	la vague
well (adv)	i'est mue	bien
well (n)	l'pis	le puits
west	vaie	ouest
what about it?	tiecquenais?	comment?
what do you say?	tiecq'teu'dis?	que dîtes-vous?
where?	y'ou q'chaie?	où?
whiting (fish)	l'luc	le merlan
why not?	pourtyi pas?	pourquoi pas?
winnow	venteu l'grain	vanner
woodcock	l'videco	la bécasse
wool	la fi	la laine
worry (v)	talbateu	tourmenter
wren	l'riberte	le roitelet
yellow wagtail	l'laboréu	la printanière
yes	vied'à, ouai	oui
young	jaunne	jeune

BIBLIOGRAPHY

HISTORICAL

Ansted, D. T. and Latham, R. C. *The Channel Islands* (3rd edn 1893)

Cachemaille, J. L. V. *The Island of Sark* (1874-5, revised and edited by Laura E. Hale, 1928)

De Carteret, A. R. *The Story of Sark* (Guernsey, 1956)

—. and Ewen, A. H. *The Fief of Sark* (Guernsey, 1969)

De Schickler, F. *Les Eglises de Refuge en Angleterre* (Paris, 1892)

Dupont, Gustave. *Histoire du Cotentin et de ses Iles* (Caen. 1870-85)

Gerville, Le Comte de. *Iles du Cotentin* (France, 1846)

Le Huray, C. P. *The Bailiwick of Guernsey* (1952)

Le Lievre, Matthieu. *Le Méthodisme dans les Iles de la Manche* (Paris, 1885)

Marshall, Michael. *Hitler Invades Sark* (Guernsey, undated)

Pitts, J. Linwood. *Witchcraft and Devil Lore in the Channel Islands* (Guernsey, 1886)

Selosse, Louis, *L'Ile de Serk, un état féodal au XXe siècle* (Lille, 1911, 1928)

Toyne, S. M. *Sark, a Feudal Survival* (Eton, 1959)

Tremayne, Julia. *Mrs Tremayne's Diaries* (1979)

Tupper, F. B. *The History of Guernsey and its Bailiwick* (Guernsey, 1854)

Wood, A. and M. *Islands in Danger* (1955)

Newspapers, and periodicals and papers

Comet, Evening Press and *Star* (all Guernsey)

Sark Greffe records

Société Guernesiaise, La. *Records and Transactions* (from 1882, annual)

Société Jersiaise, La. *Bulletins Annuels* (from 1875)

ARCHAEOLOGY

Kendrick, T. D. *The Archaeology of the Channel Islands,* vol I (1928)

GEOLOGY

Adams, C. J. D. *A geochronological and related isotropic study of rocks from north-western France and the Channel Islands (United Kingdom)* (unpubl. D. Phil thesis, Univ of Oxford, 1967)

Gibbons, Wes. *Rocks of Sark* (Jersey, 1975)

Hill, E. 'The rocks of Sark, Herm and Jethou', *Quart, Jl Geol Soc London,* line rocks of Sark', *Quart Jl Geol Soc London,* 48, 112-47.

—. and Bonney, T. G. 'On the hornblende-schists, gneisses and crystalline rocks of Sark', *Quart Jl Geol Soc London* , 48, 112-47

Mourant, A. E. and Warren, J. R. 'Minerals and Mining in the Channel Islands', *Soc Guernesiaise Trans* (1933)

Plymen, G. H. 'A preliminary survey of the geology of Sark', *Geol mag,* 63, 255-64.

Sutton, J. and Watson, J. 'The Structure of Sark, Channel Islands', *Proc Geol Ass,* 68, 179-203

Woolridge, S. W. 'The petrology of Sark', *Geol Mag,* 62, 241-52.

NATURAL HISTORY

Bichard, J. D. and McClintock, David. *Wild Flowers of the Channel Islands* (1975)

Dobson, Roderick. *The Birds of the Channel Islands* (1952)

Jee, Nigel. *Guernsey's Natural History* (Guernsey, 1968)

McClintock, David. *The Wild Flowers of Guernsey* (1975)

Marquand, E. D. *Flora of Guernsey and the lesser Channel Islands* (1901)

Rountree, F. R. G. *Birds of Sark* (Sark, 1974)

Supplement to Birds of Sark, 1991

Periodicals and papers

Le Sueuer, F. and McClintock, D. 'Check-list of flowering plants and Ferns wild on Sark', *Soc Guern Trans* (1962)

Long, R. 'Rhopalocera (Lep) of the Channel Islands', *Entomologist's Gazette* (Nov 1970)

Luff, W. A. 'The Insects of Sark', *Soc Guern Trans* (1902)

BIBLIOGRAPHY

Shayer, C. J. 'Sark butterflies', *Soc Guern Trans* (1966)

GENERAL

Admiralty, *Channel Pilot, vol 2*
Adlard Coles, K. *Channel Harbours and Anchorages* (1956)
Bowles, Mrs Henry. *Sark—the Gem of the Channel Islands* (1908)
Carey, E. F. and Wimbush, H. B. *The Channel Islands* (1904)
Clark, Leonard, *Sark Discovered (1956, rev edn 1971)*
Gueret, Yvonnick and Armel *L'Ile de Sercq* (1973)
Hathaway, Sibyl M. *Dame of Sark* (1961)
Jellicoe, G. B. *A Landscape Plan for Sark* (Sark, 1967)
Kennedy, Peter. *Folk songs of Britain and Ireland* (1975)
Latrobe, G. and L. *Guide to the Coast, Caves and Bays of Sark* (Guernsey, 1914, rev edn, 1964)
Lockley, R. M. *The Charm of the Channel Islands* (1950)
Marshall, Michael. *Sark* (Guernsey, undated)
Platt, Ernest. *Sark as I found it (1935)*
Stoney, Barbara. *Sibyl Dame of Sark* (1978)
Toplis, W. A. and Oxenham, J. *The Book of Sark* (1908)
Woolnough, W. B. *Scrambles in Sark* (1861)

FICTION

Dobree, L. E. *Underneath the Surface*
Gallienne, Robin E. *At the Leap of San Juan* (1898)
Hathaway, Sibyl M. *Maid of Sark* (1939)
Hugo, Victor. *Toilers of the Sea*
Kaye-Smith, Sheila. *The George and the Crown*
Lane, Louisa. *Sark Legends (c 1850)*
Neele, H. *The Romance of History* (c. 1880)
Oxenham, John. *Carette of Sark* (1907)
—. *A Maid of the Silver Sea*
—. *Pearl of Pearl Island* (1908)
—. *The Perilous Lovers*
Peake, Mervyn. *Mr Pye* (1953)
Philips, A. *Somewhere in Sark* (c. 1920)
Stretton, Hesba. *The Doctor's Dilemma* (c 1860)
Tickell, Jerrard. *Appointment with Venus* (1946)
Volk, Gordon. *Cliffs of Sark* (undated)

170

POETRY

Blakemore, Trevor, *Elementals* (1935), *Moonset* (1924), *Poems* (1955), *Poems & Ballads* (1912), *Star-dust* (undated), *Storm* (undated), *Sunrise* (1933)
Swinburne, A. C. *Collected Poems*
Vos, George H. *Sargia* (undated)

DRAMA

Douglas-Home, William. *The Dame of Sark* (1974)
Slade, Julian and Reynolds, Dorothy. *Free as Air* (musical)

ACKNOWLEDGMENTS

M Y sincere thanks for the 'specialist' assistance of David McClintock (flora), Dr Clive Bishop (geology), Eric W. Sharp (marine history), the late Philip Carré (patois), the late Frank Rountree and the late Philip J. Guille (ornithology), the late Dame Sibyl Hathaway and Michael Beaumont (seignory), the late Leonard Matchan and Sue Groves (Brecqhou), Ann Blakemore, who loaned her late husband's unpublished MS, David Johnston (archaeology), Roger Brehaut (natural history), Hilary Carré, the late Hubert Lanyon and the staffs of the Guille-Allés and Priaulx libraries. I am also grateful to the Geological Association for their permission to reproduce the Sutton and Watson map.

Others whose generous help was invaluable include Alfie Adams, the late Dave and Maude Adams, Dick and Wendy Adams, the late Dina Baker, the late Jehanne and Harry Bell, Joyce Betty, May Carré, Johnny de Carteret, Lawrence de Carteret, Rossford de Carteret, Ruth de Carteret, Rev and Mrs Cecil Deeks, Marie de Garis, Doug Falby, May Falle, Pat Falle, the late Reggie Falle, Geoffrey Gosselin, the late John Guille, the late Jim Hamon, John Hamon snr and jnr, Harriet and the late Philip Hamon, Trevor Hamon, Monica Herry, Martin Joyner, Trevor Kendall, the late Sam Langford and Vicky Langford, John La Trobe-Bateman, the late Elizabeth Le Feuvre, Phyllis and the late Jack Le Feuvre, Maria Marsden, David Melling, Guy Messenger, the late Capt. Ronald C. Morton, Denis Norris, Philip Perrée jnr. and sen., Lawrence Roberts, Tom and the late Ann Sutcliffe, Michael Terry, Michael Thorpe, Reg Titford, Pat Toplis, the late Cyril Wakley and John York.

Inadvertently I may have omitted others whose kindness confirmed my affection for Sark and its people. My apologies to them—and a final thank you for the original motivation and sustained progress successfully spurred by Boots.

INDEX